What Did I Do in the Bar

Joe Nelis: A Memoir

Joe Nelis

Colmcille Press

Published December 2020 by
COLMCILLE PRESS
Ráth Mór Centre
Bligh's Lane
Derry BT48 0LZ
www.colmcillepress.com

Copyright © Joe Nelis/Colmcille Press.

The author asserts his moral rights in this work in accordance with the Copyright, Designs and Patents Act 1998.

Edited by Garbhán Downey
Layout/design by Joe McAllister, Hive Studios – www.hivestudio.org

A CIP catalogue record for this book is available from the British Library.

ISBN 978 1 914009 03 7

All rights reserved. No part of this publication may be reproduced, distributed, or transmitted in any form or by any means, including photocopying, recording, or other electronic or mechanical methods, without the prior written permission of the author/publisher, except in the case of brief extracts/samples embodied in factual/academic reviews and certain other non-commercial uses permitted by copyright law.

Author's Note: I have written these stories of real events. Most of them occurred in the bars I worked. Others were incidents while I worked as a doorman, or in different settings. This is just one barman's story.
Joe Nelis, December 2020

*For Peter, Brian and Kevin
who, as children, and now adults,
we love and are proud of.
I hope they enjoy it.*

Brandywell Pride, 1949

I was born at 23 Brandywell Avenue on the fourth of November 1949 at 6.10pm. The time of my birth probably relates to my love for tea.

My parents were William and Margaret Nelis, known to our neighbours as Big Bill and Maggie. My father was a shoemaker and had a repair shop on the Lecky Road. My mother was a full-time mother; I was the second youngest of thirteen children, seven of whom lived. My parents lost two sets of twins after they were each only a few months old; my sister Annie died during a small operation in hospital and Jim died after when he was just a few days old.

I had four brothers – Billy, Jim (II), Johnny and Harry, and two sisters, Margaret and Sadie.

As my siblings got older, my mother started working again in Tillie's Factory, where she remained for years. I remember as a young child going down with my older brother Harry to my father's shop with tea and sandwiches. He had a large grandfather clock behind the counter with no hands on the face. There was a sign on the clock, 'No tick here'. It was a joke, of course, as the vast number of customers to the shop had two or three pairs of their children's shoes being repaired at any given time. My father was a big football fan and was a member of the Derry & District League Committee. At night, after he came home from the shop and got a bite to eat, he would sit on the floor with a last and would repair any of the footballers' boots who called to the house – Johnny Campbell, Eddie and Jobby Crossan, Jim McLaughlin and many more.

My brother Billy played for Derry City and Coleraine and Johnny played for Sligo Rovers. This was something which brought great pride to my father – and mother, as she was a big football fan also.

My mother's father was James Taggart, union man. James was also a big football fan and, along with a couple of local men, built the Foyle Harps Hall on Hamilton Street. They formed a local youth football team, Foyle Harps, who went on to become the most successful junior team in the city, winning nine McAlinden Cup Finals, the Blue Riband trophy in the D&D.

My Granda James ran dances and a movie night to raise funds for the hall and the team. My mother sewed the first football rig.

My father was from Foster's Terrace on the Lecky Road. My parents met at one of the dances in the Harps Hall, and two years later they were married. While my mother and father were engaged, my father had sat an exam for the Police Academy and received word that he had passed the exam. He went to Omagh for a fitness and medical test. A week later he received a letter to report to the academy in Omagh, as he had been accepted.

That night after work, he went up with a spring in his step to let my mother hear his news. He had not told my mother about his application, as no one he knew from his area had ever been successful before. He felt that, now he was getting married, this would ensure a better-paid job and a more stable future for them both.

He knocked on my Granda's door, on Brandywell Road, and my mother appeared to see my father with a smiling face.

'Maggie, I have been accepted into the Police Academy in Omagh. I am going to be a policeman.'

My mother just stared at him. 'Come in, Bill,' she said after a few seconds.

My father stepped into the living room where my Granda James was sitting by the fire smoking his pipe. My mother told Granda the news.

My Granda put down his pipe and sat in silence.

'What is wrong, James?' my father asked. 'Are you not happy for us?'

My Granda got up and stood opposite my father – not face to face, as my Granda was about five foot nine and my father was six foot six.

'Bill,' he said, 'there is no other fella in this town that I would pick to marry Maggie over you. Nobody. I have seen what some policemen have done in my time, and I don't want a son-in-law who has anything to do with the police, and that's my last word about it.'

My father turned to my mother and saw the distraught look on her face. He then turned back to James, who had sat down and lifted his pipe again. 'Excuse us a minute, James,' he said. And my mother and father went out to the front hall.

'Just tell me, Maggie, what you want me to do – that's all that matters to me.'

'I just want us to get married and be happy, but I don't want my father to resent you for this decision, Bill.'

'That's fine, Maggie, I love shoemaking anyway.'

They went back into Granda, and my father told him he was sticking to the shoe job. My father, being the honest man that he was, added, 'Not because I felt I would have to give it up for fear of you, James. It's my love for Maggie and my respect for your feelings, James.'

And so, they were married on the fourth of August 1929 in St Columba's Church, Long Tower.

* * *

As a child, 'the Brandy', as we called it, was a great place to live. Our house was just two doors from the Brandywell football ground and on Saturdays of home games the queue would be lined up at the turnstile just up from our porch. The famous Sammy Coyle would be there with his apple cart, selling to the fans as they waited to get in. His famous sales patter, 'Beautiful American apples, straight from Portadown' could be heard all over the avenue.

On a Friday, Sammy would come around in an old Ford van selling fresh herring and other fish. Six fish for two shillings. Nobody ate meat on a Friday then. His sales cry was: 'Fresh herring, fresh herring, no sooner in your belly, till it's muscle on your back.'

There was another man who came around the area often. He was injured in the war and was in a wheelchair. He had a grindstone wheel attached to the side of the chair, and he sharpened knives and forks for sixpence. The summer days were spent up on the Soldiers' Banking off Bishop Street and sometimes in Gilmartin's Orchard, which was where Bluebell Gardens is today.

The Harps hall became a band hall as well when the Owen Roe O'Neill Brass and Flute Band was formed. A number of years later, a second band emerged, The Wolfe Tone Brass and Silver Band. They build a new hall at the back of Southend Park, and another, the Lady of Lourdes Hall, at the top of the Brandy. Built by the people of the area for the people, it was the first real community hall. It had it all – dances, films, shows, concerts, a children's club, basketball and table-tennis. It was magic for everyone.

I remember one afternoon, just before I started going to school, a team of basketball players from the American Naval Base in Derry came to the hall to play a club select team in a challenge match. After the match was over, the Americans were standing outside the hall smoking, waiting for their lift back to the base. The van came and they stepped on their cigs and climbed into the van. Some of the local lads lifted the large ends and lit them. I thought I was a big boy and lifted one and got a light. I nearly died coughing and all the lads had a good laugh but I still kept puffing. When I got finished I went straight down the street to our house.

When I got home, my mum grabbed me, and I thought I was dead for smoking. 'Joe,' she said, 'we got word today, you start school on Monday.'

I was delighted, not about school – rather about not getting smacked.

She said, 'You know what this means, Joe?'

'Yes,' I replied, 'I have to be good.'

'Yes, Joe,' she said, 'and you have to give up smoking.'

Monday morning, my first day of school. Up to the Wee Nuns at the Long Tower. The head nun at the front door to greet all the new starters. 'Hello Mrs Nelis, and who is the lovely boy?' she asked.

'This is Joseph,' my mother replied.

'Hello, Joseph. And has he any other names, Mrs Nelis?'

'Yes, Aloysius, sister.'

'Oh,' she said, 'I'm Sister Aloysius.'

I burst out crying and said to my mother, 'That's not funny. Why did you give me a girl's name?'

I never knew Saint Aloysius was a Jesuit priest from the sixteenth century.

Sister Aloysius was a real saint; I never once saw her get angry or slap a child in the three years I was there. She didn't just teach children about Christianity, she showed you how to live it every day.

When I was eight, I moved to the Christian Brothers Brow of the Hill School on the Lecky Road. There was on a different planet from the Wee Nuns. The age range, from eight to fifteen years old, meant that there was a bit of bullying in the playground at lunchtime. Also, for the two years, my brother Harry was still there, so I was fine, but I knew once Harry would leave I would have to harden up – or hide. And it's difficult to hide in a playground with two hundred children looking on.

The staff were a mix of Brothers and lay teachers; no women ever taught there. I knew some of the boys got a hard time from some of the teachers, but I didn't get any bother to tell you the truth. Harry knew most of the older boys, so I never got any trouble with them.

When we were about ten, we were all expected to attend Gaelic football training, three times a week, in Celtic Park at 4.00pm after school. Saturday was still the highlight of my week, going to the Derry City matches. The atmosphere was great, especially when it was Glentoran or Linfield. The crowds then were massive, up to 10,000 but all standing. When we started to play in the schools league, we travelled to different grounds to play. In 1963, we travelled to Croke Park to play in the final of the Under-15 Schools All Ireland. We beat De La Salle School from Dublin – the first time ever a school from Derry won it. Tom McGuinness, Martin's brother, was captain, and other players I remember were Dom Moore and Andy Quigley.

A funny thing happened a week later. We were all brought into a classroom and were told by a member of the GAA committee that, as long as we were playing Gaelic, we were not allowed to go to a soccer match or play for any football teams. I was picked out and told that my brother Billy was playing for Derry City and I had been seen at all the matches – and that this would not be allowed any more.

'So,' I replied, 'it's all right for you to sit in the Brandywell Stand with your father, because your father is chairman of Derry City. I can't go with my father, as he is dead, but now you're telling me I can't go to watch my brother? No chance. Keep your Gaelic.'

And I never played another game! Early retirement.

My father died of a heart attack on my eleventh birthday in November 1960. From then on, my eldest brother Billy became my lifetime hero. After I packed in the Gaelic, I went everywhere Billy and also my brother Johnny were playing, especially the summer cup competitions.

The Wolfe Tone Band, over in Southend Park, were now a class outfit and winning prizes. Each Sunday afternoon, they would have a band practice from 3.00pm to 5.00pm. Non-members were allowed to sit in and listen. After practice, a few of the band would sit on and have a small session where they would play Glenn Miller classics.

I loved the big sound and could not take my eyes off the drummers. I loved music from as young I can remember. As a child of four or five, I would go to a neighbour's house, Mrs Fox's, and she had record player and lots of classical music and scores from the musicals. When we were in the house, she would play my favourite, Intermezzo, from Cavellaria Rusticana by Mascagni. My mother and Mrs Fox probably had a good laugh at my dancing.

After I gave up Gaelic, I was coming home one night with a pal of mine. I heard this music coming from a shed on the Lecky Road. The door was open and we had a look in. It was the bandhall of Saint Mary's Accordion Band. The man who was in charge was Willie Healy from Ann Street.

I sat and watched the two drummers. One was Willie's son, William, and the other was an elderly man called George Hasson. George had been a drummer in the Royal Marines Band, and he had taught William. I was hooked and joined the next night. I could hardly settle in school each day, waiting to get down to practice with George each night, and I loved it, every second.

Within a couple of weeks, I had made it into the band and got my uniform. We were travelling to different towns all through the summer on a bus. At each town or village, we would stop at the edge of the town, assemble, and then march through the town to the other end. As we played, members who had not yet got into the band and volunteers would walk through the town with collection boxes. The bus would be waiting at the end of town and we would drive then to the next town.

I wondered when I started with St Mary's Band, why we learned tunes like Derry's Walls and The Green Grassy Slopes of the Boyne, not to mention God Save the Queen. All would become clear before long. On road trips, when passing the likes of Coleraine and Limavady, we would then belt these tunes out and make a pretty good collection. This was the band's main source of income.

My favourite trips were to Bundoran, and we always got a few hours to ourselves in the town before heading back. Sometimes if you were really lucky, you might even get a kiss off a girl sitting beside you on the way home. A number of fellas met their girlfriends in the band and went on to get married.

Sometimes, on my way home, I would meet lads from the Wolfe Tone Band, and they would slag me about not joining my local band.

'I just wanted to join the best band in Derry,' I would tell them. And the slagging would go on – but all good banter and times.

I loved growing up in the Brandy. One of the old customs – now dying out – was that so many people then had nicknames – names like Beaver O'Reilly, Noodles McCann, Doc Doherty, Stout Ferguson, Yankee Kerr, Jalex Bradley. These were not derogatory names but were used by their best friends, nearly as a kind of bonding.

The neighbours were the best of people from the two Mulholland sisters, retired nurses, who looked after all the ailments and accidents in the street, to Jackie Curran, our next-door neighbour, and first in the street to own a car, and would take anyone to hospital when needed. It's unbelievable now, but we knew the names of every family in the five streets in the Brandywell area.

Growing up in the Brandywell, 1950s-60s

One of my best memories as a child was when my father and my uncle, Dan Moyne, took me to see Billy 'Spider Junior' Kelly fight McCarthy in the King's Hall in Belfast. Kelly was defending his British and Commonwealth title. Dan took us up in his new car, a Vanguard.

Kelly won on points after fifteen rounds. The excitement was unbelievable as the Kellys were from the Brandy. One of our own.

On the way back from Belfast, Dan stopped at the Ponderosa Bar on Glenshane Mountain for some refreshments. My father asked the barman for a packet of cigs. There were none on the shelf.

'I have to go down to the cellar, Bill,' he said to my father. 'Do you want to come down and see the cellar – I don't think you've been down yet?'

'Great,' my father replied.

'Bring the wee boy down with you.'

I was up off my seat and took my father's hand as we went down the cellar steps. There were all kinds of crates and bottles, seats, and a large amount of white bags, stacked in piles against the walls.

My father asked, 'What's in all the bags?'

'Salt, Bill, bags of salt.'

'You must sell some salt,' my father smiled.

'Me, Bill? I don't sell salt, but the guy who sold it to me, he could sell salt.'

I never caught on to his answer till years later.

The next day, Billy Kelly was paraded through Derry on the back of a lorry, with his Lonsdale Belt, and thousands lined the streets

* * *

My mother and father had a strong religious belief. The Rosary every night at home after our tea, Confession every month, and Mass on Sundays. My father was a great believer in going to Mass and Communion on the first Friday of the month. On the Thursday night before Friday the fourth of November 1960, which would be my eleventh birthday, my father and I went to Confession.

The next morning, he and I went to Mass at 7.00am and received Communion. We went home and had our breakfast, then he left me at the school gate where he handed me a ten-shilling note: 'This will get you sweets for your birthday. I have left you a present on top of the glass cabinet. I didn't want you to bring it to school.'

I felt great and watched him as he walked down the Lecky Road to his work on the docks. My father had given up the shoe shop, because plastic shoes were getting popular as they were cheaper than leather, but my father wouldn't touch them as he believed they would harm children's feet.

I didn't go home for lunch as my mother was working in Tillie's Factory at this time. I spent the money on sweets for me and my friends at school. At 3.30pm, I came down the walk from my classroom and towards the main gate. My oldest brother, Billy, was waiting for me, and he was standing beside a big black car.

Billy came forward and put his arm around me and told me to get into the car. He got me settled and then told me our father had taken a heart attack and was very ill in hospital. The car then was driven by the driver up to the Long Tower Girls School to lift my younger sister Sadie.

When Sadie got into the car, Billy took us to our brother's house. Johnny and his wife Lily were living in Meadowbank Avenue. Lily brought us in and then Billy told us our father had died. Lily comforted us as Billy had to leave and tell the rest of our family the news.

That night, Johnny and Lily took us up home. As we walked into our house in the Brandy, my father's coffin took up the length of the whole wall. That was the first thing I noticed. As Sadie and I stood looking at my father's remains, we just cried and could not stop. When my mother moved us away, she stood me in front of the glass cabinet, against the other wall. There on top of the cabinet sat an open box containing a beautiful fisherman's knife, with a pearl handle. My father knew I loved fishing, out the line [an old railway line that ran along the bank of the river Foyle], on Letterkenny Road.

My father was buried two days later, on the Sunday at 2.30pm. The funeral cortege was one of the longest I have ever seen. I clearly remember Sadie and I were directly behind the hearse. As we were walking up through the cemetery, we looked down on Brandywell Road, and the mourners were still coming up the road.

The next day, Monday, was when the Requiem Mass was held at 10.00am. Again, there was a large crowd for the Mass. As we left the church, after the Mass, I met one of the Christian Brothers, who was at the Mass.

'Don't forget, Joe, your exam is at 9.00am tomorrow out in Templemore School on the Northland Road.'

'Yes, Sir,' was all that I could say. I never liked that Brother after that, mind you he was never one of my favourites at any time.

The next day, I got up at 7.00am, and got washed and dressed. I never told any of my family that I was sitting the 11-Plus exam. As I was leaving the house at 8.00am, my mother was sitting crying with my older sister Margaret. I remember walking out the Northland Road and wondering why we were being sent to a Protestant school to sit an exam when they got to do it in their own schools.

I finally got there and stood around till we were taken into a classroom. All I could think of was my mother and Margaret sitting there crying. I didn't hear one word that the teacher said. Then he rang a bell and told us to begin. I turned the papers over but could not see a word; my eyes were full of tears. I just wanted to get home to my mother. I just sat staring at the paper and got more and more upset.

Finally, after about thirty minutes, I lifted my paper and walked up and sat it on the teacher's desk. He looked at it and told me to sit down and start writing. I told him I was going home and walked out.

I ran most of the way home and my mother, Margaret and Sadie were there. I told them I didn't do the exam and I didn't care about it.

* * *

My mother's brother James had a farm in Omagh. Every year, James would come down with his wife Mary, and their daughter Marie, and they would stay for a few days. James was a great storyteller, and it was taken for granted that we would all gather in our house at night to listen to his stories. Even as a thirteen-year-old, I was enthralled by the stories.

Even my older brothers never missed a night. I remember one story he told us when I was older, and it just stuck in my head. He had a lot of cows and had a bull. Farmers who only had a few cows would borrow the bull off James for a week for the breeding season. One farmer had not returned the bull after the week, so James went to see why. As James was walking up the road to the farmer's house, he heard this loud shouting coming from a field on the other side of the ditch. James climbed up onto the ditch and looked into the field. There was the farmer and he was behind the plough. The bull was pulling the plough up the field, and the farmer shouting to the bull: 'Get up there, ye boy ye. I'll teach you there's more to life than sex.'

James was going to choke him and he never got the bull again.

A few years later, James sold the farm and moved to Bundoran where he bought a bed & breakfast and shop. On a day excursion with the school, I called to visit him and his family. He kept me up for six weeks holidays. I had a great time at the B&B home. I helped each day, making the beds with his wife Mary and cleaning the rooms in the morning. Then after lunch, I would work in the shop with James. At 6.00pm we would have our dinner, and then James would give me some money to go out to the amusements for a couple of hours or go down to the beach. I loved going for a run on the donkeys up and down the beach. Then up to the amusements and getting a large 99 ice cream, then back for 9.00pm.

The B&B was always full with holiday-makers or business reps. Each night, James would sit in the living room with some of the residents, usually the reps as the holiday-makers would be out on the town. James would offer them tea, coffee, Horlicks or a wee drink. Then he would start telling his stories. Looking back now, I don't remember any guest leaving the room early, even when it was getting late. And when James was ready for bed, they would often ask: 'Just one more story, James.'

I remember one night in particular, we were all sitting cosy in the room, and James was telling a story. James never closed his front door till he was going to bed. Suddenly, this man walked into the hallway and opened the room door and sat down beside James. James just carried on with the story. When he finished, he asked the man would he like a cup of tea. He said he would. James went to the kitchen where his wife Mary was. James made the tea, and May went into the shop.

James came in with the tea and some biscuits. I had never seen this man before, and it was not like James not to introduce any of his friends who called in regularly at night. There was something odd about this man's manner and demeanour. He never spoke a word. James just smiled at us all, as if to say, don't worry, it's all right.

James started another story, and the stranger hung on every word from James. About ten minutes later, four men in white coats and a Garda officer came through the front door and into the living room. They told the man they had come to bring him home. He got very agitated but James assured him that there was nothing to fear or to worry about.

James walked him out to the hospital van at the door. It turned out that the man had escaped from a local mental hospital, where he was being treated for a mental health condition. James had heard earlier that day that a man had escaped from the hospital and had done a large amount of damage on the way out. James had guessed when the man came in that it was the patient. When James went out to make the tea, he told Mary to phone the hospital and that he would keep the man in his home until they arrived.

James was a really cool man, never panicked for a minute. It also made me more aware – James doesn't make up these stories. I have great memories of those nights with James and his family, and the music nights with his close friends.

* * *

As I have already stated, my father's family were from Foster's Terrace on the Lecky Road. My father had a younger brother, Johnny. Johnny was like a twin of my father, except in stature. Johnny was only 5'6". He was always dressed to perfection, with a three-piece suit and his chain watch in his waistcoat pocket. He was always known as Squire Nelis.

Johnny loved his cigarettes and a bottle of stout, and was afraid of nothing – except his big sister Lizzie. Lizzie was my aunt, who always brought great company to my mother after my father's death. She was really funny and a beautiful singer. During the First World War, Lizzie was sitting on the steps of Tillie's Factory, having a tea-break. Suddenly, from a lorry going across the bridge, she heard fifteen-year-old Johnny shouting to her from the lorry: 'I'm going to the train for Belfast – I've signed up for the army.'

Lizzy got a truck driver from the factory to take her to the station and told the officer-in-charge Johnny's age. Then, when she got him into the truck, she battered him all the way home. Years later, Johnny told us he was more afraid of Lizzie that he was of the Germans.

One year later Johnny ran away again and managed to join up at sixteen. My father could not believe it when he heard what had happened as Johnny looked like a wee boy. Small as he was, Johnny boxed for the army team and played hockey for the army team as well. When the war was over, Johnny came back with five medals and a keepsake of a bayonet and scabbard.

In the early 1950s, Uncle Johnny would visit us often. One day, I noticed that Johnny's arm was badly scarred. After he left, I asked my father what happened the arm – had he been shot?

When Johnny signed up, they were in a camp in Belfast, waiting to be shipped to England for training. They were in tents, and there was a big half-barrel burning wood and coke. The men were standing around arguing who were the bravest, the Belfast men or the Derry men. Some were doing somersaults and jumping over sticks men would hold up. Others were doing push-ups etc. Johnny got fed up listening to them. He got up and walked over the barrel, lifted it off the ground and swung it in the air.

'Beat that,' he said, and then collapsed in a heap with the pain.

He spent three weeks in the Mater Hospital and on his release he was shipped out to England the following night. His family were not even informed that he was in hospital with severe burns. My father said he probably would not them contact his family in case Lizzie would come up for him.

When my Granda James took ill after his second wife died, only four years after they were married, Lizzie, who was not married, went up to look after my Granda, and a few years later they were married. So my aunt became my step-granny. All legal, but still a rare occurrence.

* * *

After father passed away, my mother was sick for months and could not work. At that time, there were only my mother, Margaret, Harry, Sadie and me living in the house. Harry had just started serving his time as a joiner so Margaret was the only one bringing in a wage. Sadie and Margaret took over the running of the house. Margaret and Harry were working each day, so Sadie and I did the odd jobs. Sadie was only ten at the time but was as good as a twenty-year-old; making me and my mother a lunch every day and cups of tea for my brothers that were married and calling in every day.

Margaret made our dinner at night after work. She also brought home bag of shirts to work on when we went to bed, to get some extra money.

* * *

Up in Quarry Street lived Johnny Holmes, the Brandywell entrepreneur. Johnny had a horse and cart and when old houses were being demolished, Johnny would take all the wooden rafters, slates and any metal objects away on his cart. Johnny had about twenty young helpers from the area. When he brought the cart back to Quarry Street, he would take it around the back lane of his house to a large shed. There was where the work was done. The roof tiles would be carefully set in piles. These would be sold for repairing broken slates in any homes being repaired. The rafters would be carried into the shed. Then, we would set about sawing the rafters into pieces, which were then cut into sticks with hatchets which the older lads handled. A few lads would sit cutting up bicycle tubes into two-inch strips to use as elastics to tie the bundles of sticks. Then the bundles were piled in dozens. It was like an assembly line, and it was great fun.

When it was all done and dusted, each lad got a small four-wheel, four-sided trolley and would stack it with as many bundles of sticks as could fit, usually three dozen. Then we all headed out to different streets and sold the sticks, a penny a bundle, twelve for a shilling. Johnny took all the metal to the scrap yard by cart. We might have two shillings for our work, but more than that, we enjoyed it. And at that time, two shillings got you a fish supper, coke and a little change.

* * *

I was still going to matches on a Saturday. Billy was now playing for Coleraine. Him and Fay Coyle had moved there as Derry were paying them less than the players signed from the Republic's league. At this particular match Coleraine were playing at the Brandywell, Jim, Johnny, Harry and I were all standing together in the unreserved end of the ground. Johnny had had a wisdom tooth removed at the dentist and was still bleeding and in pain.

Every time that Billy or Fay touched the ball, the crowd gave them awful stick. About fifteen minutes into the match, Coleraine got a corner and Billy took it, and big Fay went up like a swan and buried it in the back of the Derry net. The Coleraine supporters cheered, while the Derry fans went mad. There were men standing beside us and they started shouting obscenities at Billy and Fay. I could see my brothers were getting wired up. A few minutes later, Billy threw a long pass down the middle to Fay and kept running to the Derry eighteen-yard line. Fay dummied the Derry right back and square the ball across the box to Billy, who met it in full flight and nearly busted the Derry net.

That was like a knife to the Derry fans. The men beside us went ballistic, calling Billy and Fay everything under the sun. The next time Billy touched the ball, one man beside us shouted: 'Break the bastard's leg.'

Johnny tried to tell him to shut up but he could not make out what Johnny was saying. Again, he started shouting at Billy. Suddenly, Johnny punched him full on and he just dropped.

Then Jim turned to the others standing around us and said: 'And if we hear another threat from you lot, it won't be Billy leaving with a broken leg.'

I was shaking but none of them opened their mouths about Billy or Fay after that. Fay scored again in the second half and Coleraine won three-one.

When I was twenty-something, I went up to Coleraine to help Billy finish a job; Billy had his own steel business then. I could not believe the number of people who knew him from his days playing for Coleraine. I swear, it was like walking along the streets with a star. Even when we went in for something to eat, none of the places took any money. As a worker and a businessman, Billy was always straight and honest. After my father died, Billy always looked out for me and the rest of our family. My hero for sure, I never needed the cinema stars – I had our Billy.

* * *

I remember when Gilmartin's orchard started to get pulled down. It was to make way for the new houses in Bluebell Hill Gardens. All the kids in the area were gutted. This was our cowboy land where we fought the Indians; where as cops we caught the baddies; where we climbed the trees like Tarzan; or just sat in our own gang telling ghost stories. We were so sad about the loss of 'our' orchard that when the houses were built we didn't even like the families who lived there. So we moved our gang to the Soldier's Banking, behind Johnny Holmes's house. It was a large rock quarry with a flat grassy top. Great for football but a long way down if the ball went over the side. It stretched from Quarry Street across to the bottom of Bishop Street.

We would often challenge the Bishop Street gang to a match. Often as not, it would end up in a fight but, at our age, nobody ever got hurt. It was mainly a fight with intended missed punches. Five minutes later we were all friends again – till the next match.

At the Christian Brothers School, some of my friends lived in Creggan Estate. Sometimes after school, Christy McCormack, my friend John's brother, and I would go up to Creggan just to pass the time and spend a few hours with our pals. One of my friends in Creggan was Johnny McGilloway from Greenwalk. His parents bought him a set of drums as he was drumming mad.

This night, we left Johnny's after 6.00pm and decided rather than going the long way home, we would cut through the cemetery. It was just starting to get dark but we didn't even notice; we were just amazed and talking about how lucky Johnny was. We were walking down a path between rows of graves when suddenly Christy grabbed my arm. I looked at him and his eyes were ready to pop out. He pointed to a grave about three down. I looked and then I started shaking as the clay was coming up out of the grave. I then realised how dark it was getting and I was just about able to say to Christy, 'What will we do?'

Before I got an answer, Christy took off straight past the grave, and I was only a few steps behind him. As we passed the grave we saw the gravedigger throwing out the clay with his shovel. We stopped about fifty yards past the grave, and I thought my chest was going to burst. Then the two of us burst out laughing but we never went through the cemetery again.

* * *

There were a lot of pranksters around our area and they were always up to mischief. I remember one in particular. There were numerous people who swore they had seen a very tiny woman. She wore all white, had a clubbed foot and looked like a witch – and her face seemed to be illuminated. They thought she was the devil.

Within a few days, this woman had been seen in different areas. Women were even afraid to go out at night, even to the corner shops. She was spotted by passers-by mostly at night, on street corners or up back lanes. Then one night a crowd gathered as she stood in the back alley that led from Brandywell Avenue to Southend Park. She never moved when the crowd gathered. Just the white figure with the lit-up face, standing still, facing the crowd. Suddenly, she came running towards the crowd, pulling off the shawl around her shoulders and dropping the flashlight she was holding to her face. But behind her stood another white figure who pulled off their white bed sheet and shone the torch on themselves.

The first white woman was a local lad, but another young fella, who knew where he was planning to show up got himself dressed and planned to give his pal a shock. When the white woman appeared, his mate approached him from behind and tapped him on the shoulder. You can imagine his shock when he turned and saw the figure behind him and he took off like he had seen a real ghost.

The wee white woman was never spotted again.

* * *

Another time, a worker at a local undertaker's got a coffin and a hearse and convinced a mate of his to lay in the coffin. He then sat the coffin into the back of the hearse and drove it along Foyle Road.

When the people on the street saw the hearse, with the coffin, they all stood and started blessing themselves. Halfway over the Foyle Road, the coffin lid slid open and the corpse came up out of the coffin. There were men collapsed to their knees and women were squealing and blessing themselves like mad. The hearse took off like a rocket.

The next day, the driver was sacked – no surprise there. He got a warning from the police too, but that was it.

The Roadhouse

1965: MY JOURNEY BEGINS

It was five days before Christmas day, 19664. My last day at school, and I was so happy. It's not that I hated school; I was just not the studious type.

The first week in January, my older brother, Johnny, told me that the Roadhouse Bar in Bridgend was looking to start a young man as an apprentice barman. Johnny worked as a butcher during the day in James Doherty's Butcher Shop in Waterloo Place. He also worked a few nights a week as a part-time barman in the Roadhouse.

The next day I went down to see the manager. The manager, Leo Deehan, had been working in Chicago in a bar and restaurant called Bennigan's Bar and Grill rooms.

Leo's brother, Hugh (Tuchie) Deehan, owned the Abercorn Bar at the time and, when he bought the Roadhouse, Leo came home to manage it for him. I met Leo and we had a chat, and I suppose now it would be called an interview. Anyway I got the job. He told me to start the next day. Hours of work: 10.00am to 7.00pm, six days a week. Sunday: 11.00am till 3.00pm, back at 7.00m till 11pm. No days off. Pay: £1.00 per week.

When I came out of the bar, to walk home to the Brandywell, I was really excited, I don't know why. The money was not great, and I would have to walk to and from work, if I wanted to have any money, as the bus fares would have left little of my one pound

I believe the excitement came from my brother Johnny's stories about the bar. The craic, atmosphere and the characters who drank there. The thought of working in a place where people went to enjoy themselves.

The following morning I was up very early and walked to Bridgend. I spent my first day washing glasses, cleaning toilets, mopping the bar and lounge floors, topping up the shelves with beers and minerals, and sorting out the bottles and empty crates that had to be returned. Nothing like starting at the bottom. After my first week, I knew I would be at this work for the rest of my life. I loved every day going to work.

After a few weeks' working there, Leo, the manager let me work a few nights on the floor as a waiter. The tips were great and I was glad of the extra money.

The regulars were some of the best-known people in Derry. People like Billy (Spider) Kelly, who had been British and Empire boxing champion. Jimmy Monaghan, heavyweight boxer. John (Red) Doran, the head waiter, had served on the Queen Elizabeth liner. The two head barmen were big Dan Harkin, who ran the bar on the day shift – Dan had run the White Horse inn at Campsie before he came to the Roadhouse, a real legend. And then you had Billy Gallagher, the night-time head, who had worked in Chicago with Leo. Working with these men I learnt what a good barman should know. They had a few simple rules and I stuck to them.

Rule 1) Always show your customers respect.

Rule 2) When serving any drink make sure of a clean glass.

Rule 3) Make sure you pour a good pint.

Rule 4) Learn to make every cocktail.

Rule 5) And this was the most important, Leo told me: if you are getting bullied or threatened by any customer, report it immediately to management.

Five simple rules, but they worked then, as they still should now.

If a stranger wanted to throw his weight about, this was definitely not the bar to try it in. On the other hand, if you wanted a good night out, this was the place to come.

Whether you wanted a bit of man talk, the public bar was your spot, or if you and your wife, girlfriend, or a group of friends fancied some live entertainment, there was music five nights a week in the lounge.

Every night there were different musicians and singers. Wednesday night was Eddie (Every Voice) Kerr, who could do everyone from Al Jolson to Tom Jones. Thursday nights were country music, with performers like Ray Jordan, Jimmy Campbell, John McCready, Chuck McGuigan and Austin Rouse from Strabane, Ireland's Roger Miller. Even the great Josef Locke performed there on several occasions. I remember well his last appearance there, when he, with Mr McCafferty, performed for the last hour of the night, and he was a real performer. Their fee for the night was two free four-course meals in the restaurant upstairs, and Josef's drinks were free all night.

1967: WABBIT'S BIKE

There were many different characters in the bar as I have mentioned, but my favourite of them all was Wabbits McClean, the bike man of Derry.

He loved his bottle of stout and talking about when he was a boy hunting rabbits, but he could not pronounce the word 'rabbits' correctly, so he was known as Wabbits McClean.

Wabbits made his living by collecting scrap metal, rags, batteries, old furniture, anything he could sell to anyone who would buy it, and he removed it all with his bike.

Every Sunday night Wabbits would cycle down to the Roadhouse around nine o'clock. He would have his quota of stout, and at the end of the night, somebody with a car would put the bike in the boot and drop Wabbits home. At this time there was a new Garda Sergeant appointed for Bridgend. To say he was not popular would be true; even the station guards hated him.

The bars in Derry were closed on a Sunday but, in the Republic, bars that had a restaurant, and could serve late meals, were allowed to stay open till midnight on a Sunday night.

This particular Sunday night, the sergeant decided he would check if the Roadhouse were serving late meals to comply with the law. He arrived with a carload of Guards and marched into the bar. When he saw all the plates on the tables, and the remains of some nibbles on the plates he left. He had a look on his face that would have cut cold steel. As the Guards were walking back to the squad car, Wabbits pulled up beside the car and waved into the Guards. He knew all the regular

Guards by name. By now it was just after nine o'clock, and getting dark. The sergeant jumped out of the car and grabbed Wabbits. What do you think you are doing you scoundrel, he said to Wabbits. Poor Wabbits looked terrified. Where is your light, and your bell for this bike? Driving a bike in the dark with no bell or light, what have you to say? Poor Wabbits just left apologising: 'Sorry Sir, I will get them tomorrow, I swear.'

'If I ever see you again with them not on this bike, I will land you in gaol,' the sergeant shouted at him and got back into the car. Wabbits left the bike at home for weeks after this.

Months later the sergeant paid us another visit, and again we had the plates out on the tables. He just took a quick look in the lounge and headed back out to the car. One of the guards asked his boss: Back to the station, Sir?'

'No,' the sergeant replied, 'I want to sit in the car, and watch for a bike coming down the road.'

We followed them out, my brother, Johnny, who was now manager of the bar, and I. We knew who he was waiting on, and Wabbits still had no bell or light on the bike.

Would he bring the bike down tonight?

Just then a taxi pulled up at the door. The taxi dropped their fare off, and as he went to pull away, Johnny spoke to the driver: 'If you see Wabbits on your way to Derry, tell him the guards are waiting for him and his bike.'

'Will do, Johnny,' and he pulled away.

As the minutes passed, more and more of the patrons came out of the bar, to see this meeting. After about thirty minutes waiting, and the patrons going in and out for refills, the Guards started the car up to leave. Just as they were about to pull away, the sound of a bell could be heard clearly. It was dark by now, and no sign of a light, just a bell. The squad car stopped and the sergeant jumped out, and went straight to the middle of the main Derry road, flashlight in his hand. The bell was getting louder, but no sign of a light on the bike. By now the whole bar crowd were at the edge of the main road, waiting! Suddenly, the Guard turned the flashlight to the pathway at the side of the road. Wabbits was holding on to the handlebars with one hand, and ringing the bell for all he was worth with the other hand.

'Got you now, you thug,' the sergeant shouted at Wabbits and ran towards him. 'You're under arrest for driving a bike with no light.'

Wabbits lifted his arms up with the handlebars in them. 'What bike, Sir?' he asked.

The sergeant looked at the handlebars and we thought he was going to take a heart attack, or kill Wabbits. By now the crowd were in bits, and shouting and clapping. The Guards took off in the car, and we never saw the sergeant again. We heard later he was moved somewhere. Nobody knew where, and we cared even less.

As for Wabbits, he didn't have to buy a drink for weeks after that.

1968: NEVER SHOW FEAR

Over the next few years, there were different incidents and situations that took place in the bar. Some funny, some very serious.

Every day was a school day, just more enjoyable.

Like the night Billy Gallagher filled an empty whiskey bottle with leftover beer, from beer bottles. His wife used the beer to shampoo his children's hair, every Saturday night. Billy mentioned it kept the hair flea and dandruff free. Billy put the top back on when it was full, but sat it beside the whiskey bottles in the spirit cabinet. Billy went home that night without the bottle. The following night I was working behind the bar. During the night, the Cream of the Barley bottle on optic was empty. I reached in to the cabinet and did not even notice the seal was broken on the cork. We were so busy I didn't even notice. Some time later a customer came up to Johnny the manager. What's this craic Johnny, you selling beer for whiskey, he said, and he shook the glass, and a head appeared on the whiskey. I lifted down the whiskey from the optic, shook it, and sure enough the head appeared in full view. By now there was only about a quarter of the bottle left, and he had been the first to notice and complain.

The regular looked at me and said, 'You should sack him!'

To which Johnny replied, 'I wish I had four more like him!' And we suddenly realised what had happened the whiskey beer. Johnny put the company up a free round, and we all had a good laugh about it.

A few months later, one of my worst nights ever took place in the bar.

A few months earlier, a musician who regularly played in the bar, had suddenly lost his wife. He was devastated and left with eight children to raise on his own.

After a few months, the musicians in the town, bar staff and friends organised a concert in St Columb's Hall, with proceeds going to the family. The show was star studded, from the Clipper Carlton Showband, who were the top showband in the country, to Josef Locke, and all their services for free. All the staff had bought tickets. I was to stay and look after the bar, and my brother Harry was the doorman.

As soon as the concert was over, the staff would get taxis back to the bar, as we knew a large crowd would follow to the bar. Harry and I arrived at the bar around 7.00pm, and the staff headed to the concert. There was not one customer left in the bar.

'It's going to be a quiet night, Joe, till they get back,' Harry said. I knew they would probably be back around 10.30pm. Little did we know what was ahead of us that night.

The girls in the restaurant upstairs were getting food ready, for when the crowd returned.

Around 8.30pm, a young couple came into the bar, and that was our first customers. About fifteen minutes later, eight Belfast men came into the lounge. They ordered eight pints of stout, and asked to see the menu. They were all tall, strong-looking men. They were very loud and a bit obnoxious.

I took their drinks to their table, and they started arguing about whose turn it was to pay. At this point the bad vibes started in me, and I knew, this was not going to end well.

I tried to keep the conversation light-hearted, and said I was sure they would not want me to lose my job, if they did not pay for the drinks. They eventually paid me, and I went to get the menu. I spoke to Harry on the way, and I told him I was worried, not for just me, but the both of us.

When I came back with the menu, the comedian of the group asked me, 'Can you not count? you only brought seven pints.'

I apologised and went to get another pint. When I brought the pint down, he lifted an empty pint glass, and flung it into the open fireplace. Now, his friends started laughing, and I got really scared. I was determined that even though I was trembling, they would never see my fear. They ordered another round and I got them, and counted them on to their table, got the money, and went straight out to Harry and told him to call the Guards.

I went back in and took their food order, and tried to act normal, hoping the Guards would arrive in a few minutes.

I was taking their order to the restaurant, when Harry stopped me: 'There was a bad car accident in Buncrana, and all Guards have been sent there. It was a serious accident, and ambulances are also on their way.'

What now? I was nineteen, and Harry was twenty-two. Never did we miss our other three brothers, as much as we did now. As I went back behind the bar again, Mr Comedian said to his mates, let's just give the two boyos a few slaps, and we can take our fill of drink. It sounded like someone not wise.

This was the wakeup call for me, and when I told Harry, it was an understood rule; we were not going to take a beating laying down. Harry was a good amateur boxer, and was civil to everyone he met, but was far from soft. As for me, I thought I could beat Cassius Clay, on one of his bad nights – stupid youth.

Harry went upstairs to the cook, and told her we would send the first four up, and for her to take her time serving them.

I went in and told them the first four meals were ready, and would call the other four as soon as theirs were ready. The four went up. As they left to go up, they threw their empty glasses into the fireplace and laughed. We just wanted them split up. Harry then told me if any of the four in the lounge leave to go to the toilets, we have to get them out the back door, and I knew how he meant. After a few minutes one got up to go to the toilets, and one of his mates followed him out. Jesus, they were big men.

As the first one opened the toilet door, Harry was standing inside the toilet. Harry hit him, and he went down. The second boy turned on me but I was ready. I hit him with my left hand, 'Suzie Q' punch, and he just looked at me and lifted his fist to strike. Crack, Harry was too quick for him, and before the punch was thrown at me, Harry had put his lights out.

We dragged them out the back door and locked it. Right, Harry said, the two in the lounge next. We walked in like John Wayne, and Joe, the Wean.

'Let's go,' Harry told them, 'your friends are outside.'

They started to smile, as they got up from their chairs, but they didn't smile long. Before they were fully up, Harry landed a humdinger on the biggest one, and he went down like a sack of spuds. I hit the other guy with a decent punch, and he landed on the floor. Not knocked out, but he did not attempt to get up. I think he was afraid to get up, in case Harry hit him.

As we were getting them out, there was an awful smash of glass. The two who were out the back, climbed up on the flat roof of the bar, hoping to get into the restaurant to their friends. At that time, the bar was being redecorated, and there were tins of paint that were being used by the painters during the day, and had been left overnight on the roof. The two guys had brought down a couple of tins each, removed the lids, and were firing the tins of paint through the bar windows. Harry and I got stuck in to the boys throwing the tins. As the tins went through the windows, the couple sitting in the bar were covered in bright yellow paint, and before they had a chance to recover, another coat of white sprayed them all over. The whole commotion brought the four guys running down from the restaurant, and when they saw their mates, they made for Harry and I. I was sure we would need one of those ambulances from Buncrana shortly. The punches were flying, but with the adrenaline flowing, feeling the pain seemed oblivious. In the middle of all this, I did not even hear, or see, the taxis pulling up from the concert. Were we glad to see the cavalry? You better believe it, we were seconds away from real damage.

In a few minutes, it was all over, and the eight of them were sitting on their bums in a circle outside the bar. An hour later, the Guards arrived and they were arrested. The following morning they appeared at Buncrana court House, where they were fined for assault and damage to property. They received a large fine. The guards took them to the Bridgend border, where they were handed over to the R.U.C., and put on a train to Belfast.

They were in Derry to do a big concreting job for a week. They had finished that day, and decided to go out for a quiet drink and a meal.

Wonder what their stag parties are like?

November 3-4, 1969: Birthday Surprise

That was the year my brother Johnny, who was manager of the Roadhouse, left and went to work for the Post Office. I had finished my apprenticeship and felt I wanted a change too. A lot of the old regulars had become less frequent visitors, and I did not enjoy it as much now.

Two weeks later I got a job, full-time, in the Old City Dairy, on the Letterkenny Road.

I also took a part-time job, five nights a week, in a petrol station belonging to Conor Desmond. It was also on the Letterkenny Road, not far from the dairy.

I worked in the dairy from Monday to Friday, eight in the morning to five in the afternoon, and worked at the petrol station from Wednesday night to Sunday night from 6.00pm till midnight. I would go home from the dairy at 5.00pm to the Brandywell, grab a bite to eat, and be back at the station for 6.00pm. It was great having the extra money from the part time job as, at this time, my mother, younger sister, Sadie and I, were the only ones living at home. Mum was retired and Sadie had a full time job in Wellworths.

On this particular day, November 3, I was buzzing. The next day was my twenty-first birthday. Conor, my boss in the petrol station, was taking me for the day to Dublin, and later that night we were going to see Derry City play Shamrock Rovers in the Texaco Cup. Conor had the tickets already bought. After the match we would drive back to Derry. I had already got the day off from the dairy.

At 11.45pm, I started to close the station down. I took the readings off the pumps, and then would work out the sales, check that the reading on the till would match the sales. Then I would put the sales sheet, along with the till receipt, and cash, into a bag for Conor. Turn out all the lights, lock everything up, and Conor would collect the bag, and drop me home, about 12.30am.

On this night, I was standing in the kiosk, counting the takings in the till, when I noticed a slight movement through the glass in the kiosk. I looked up and there were four heads, with balaclavas covering them, looking in at me. One of them opened the kiosk door, and he had a gun in his hand. 'Step outside,' he said.

I stepped outside, and two of them ran me around the back of the office, where there was a small toilet, at the back of the station. When we got to the toilet door, they told me to kneel down on the step. They tied my hands to my feet, and put sellotape across my mouth. One then said to the other he would check out the front and see if the others were ready to go. When he left, the other guy pushed the gun into the back of my head, and began to speak: 'I am going to stand here for a while, and you won't know when I'm gone, and don't try anything smart, or I will blow your fucking head off. Okay?'

I nodded my head. What did he imagine I could try? I serve petrol. Did he think Harry Houdini worked here?

A minute passed, and I thought he might be gone. Then the gun was against my head again, and he spoke again: 'I'm still here you wee fucker, don't even move or I will blow your head off.'

I began to think, this bastard is enjoying this power. As he finished talking I thought I knew the voice, but no face came to me.

I sat there shaking for what seemed ages, and suddenly I heard a car take off. I prayed it was them, then threw myself backwards out of the toilet. I tried in vain to rip the tyings but they were too well tied. I had to lie on my back and push my feet against the ground, to try and slick round to the forecourt. I was also dreading that Conor might arrive in the middle of this, and get shot. Finally Conor arrived, and untied me. I told him what had happened. After he was sure I was not injured, he rang the police. As we waited for the police to come, Conor made me a hot cup of tea, in the office. I was thankful for the cup of tea, as I was now shaking from head to toe.

The police car arrived and four detectives got out of it. They were in plain clothes.

They started asking me questions. 'How many were there? What were they wearing? Had they guns? What kind of guns?' Then they would ask the same questions again in a different order. I was getting fed up with this, and just wanted time to clear my head.

Then Detective Poirot asked me, 'Do you think they were real guns?'

'Can I ask you a question?' I said. 'Have you ever seen the rows of soldiers' graves in the city cemetery?'

'Yes, I have,' he said.

'Well, a lot of them young fellas thought that the guns weren't real, that's why they are buried up there now,' I said, 'and I am going home now.'

'You will have to come to the station tomorrow, and fill out a statement,' he said.

'No he won't,' spoke Conor, 'we will do it the day after, as we are going to Dublin tomorrow, to celebrate this young man's birthday.' And with that they left.

When I got home I was still shaking. The voice of the gunman was still in my head, and I knew a face would eventually come to me.

The next day we headed to Dublin, and the news every hour gave out about the robbery. 'Four gunmen rob petrol station.' And all for £72.00 cash.

A couple of weeks later, the face to match the voice came to me, but that's for later.

January 1970: Robber Meets his Waterloo

The following January, after the robbery, there was a country music night at the Roadhouse. My best friend John McCormick and I love country music, so we decided to go. All the local country singers were putting on a full night of the best of country. We got seats as soon as we got in, as a big crowd was expected. I went up to the bar to get a couple of drinks. While I was waiting to get served, a customer seated at a table, with a couple of friends waved up to me.

Just before I had stopped working in the Roadhouse, there had been a fight outside the bar. Two guys were giving a man a hammering on the ground. My brother Harry and I rushed out and got it stopped. The man on the ground was bleeding badly, and we got him into the bar, and cleaned up. Then we got him a taxi to take him to the hospital, in case there were any bones broken. He got checked out and was fine. This was the man, now waving over to me.

I walked over and shook hands with him, and asked how he was keeping, as I had not seen him from that night. 'I'm great,' he said, 'first class, and you, Joe, how are you keeping?'

As soon as he spoke, the man with the gun's voice came back to me, sending a shiver right through me.

'I hear that you were robbed out in the garage?' he said. 'Were you scared?' And as he said it, he had a real smug smile on his face.

'Yes,' I said, 'I really was.'

'How did it feel?' he asked. He was enjoying this. The power I guessed.

His two friends were smiling away, and I knew it was definitely him.

'How did I feel?' I replied. 'A lot better than you will now.' And as I said it, I got stuck into him with both fists – I had lost it completely.

Within a minute, I was dragged off him, but his friends were afraid to touch me, as I still had a lot of good friends in the bar. John, my mate, was right by my side as usual. The regulars and staff wanted to know how it had started.

'Ask these scumbags,' I said, 'they know why. Me and my mate are leaving now, but if any of your two cronies want to finish this out in the car park, I would be more than happy.'

John and I left, and got a taxi back to Derry. Every puppy has his day.

April 1970: Lightning Strikes Twice

For the next few months after the robbery, I was constantly nervous at night in the garage. The nights were still dark, and as the cars pulled in to the station, it was hard to see who was in the car, or how many were in the car.

As the night got brighter, it became easier to see the regular customers, and the drivers of the cars. I began to feel less stress as the weeks passed. Just as I felt I was getting back to normal, it happened again.

Conor, the owner, was at a meeting that night, and after the meeting he called at McCann's Chippy in the Brandywell and arrived at the station, with two fish suppers.

We were just tucked in to the food when a car pulled in to the station.

I pulled on my work gloves and went out to serve them. The driver got out and asked me for £5.00 regular. The passenger said he needed oil and said he would get it.

'Hold on,' I said, 'I'll get it.' But he went on into the kiosk.

I knew Conor was there, no panic. As I was filling the car I was watching the clock on the pump. Suddenly from inside the kiosk, I could see Conor, standing with his hands held up above his head, and the passenger standing facing him. As I put the pump hose back on the pump, I turned on the driver and he was standing taking something out of his pocket, and it wasn't money.

I didn't even think, I punched him full on the face, and he slid down the side of the car. I dived round to the other side of the kiosk, where the door was. As I dived through the door, the robber and Conor were putting the till money into a bag, and he had Conor's wallet in his hand. I lunged at him, and grabbed the gun with both my hands. As soon as Conor realised what was happening, he punched the robber and he swayed. Then, as we struggled with him, there were two small bangs. It sounded like kids' gun firing caps.

Conor grabbed his wallet back and I grabbed the moneybag, just as his robber friend appeared, and grabbed him up, and the both of them made off.

We did not follow them, as we were not sure if the driver had another gun. We got the number of the car. The police come and ask the some questions, and I gave them a good description of the robbers, and the registration number.

The police left, and we made a cup of tea. Suddenly we both starting laughing. Imagine we didn't even notice they were using a dummy gun. While we were having the cuppa, I noticed a liquid pool on the floor. I checked where it was coming from, and it was coming from the oil cabinet. I opened the cabinet and to my shock, there were a number of the oil cans with holes in them. The gun was real, and the bullets had gone through the wooden cabinet, and through the cans of oil.

That soon took the smiles off our faces. Again, no one was arrested or charged for the robbery, and the car? It was stolen.

June 1970: No Good Deed Goes Unpunished

After the attempted robbery, I did not feel the stress. Probably because I felt like it had been a victory for Conor and I.

The summer nights were at their best, and I brought a chair out and sat in the sun. I was sitting waiting on my next customer, when the security man from the dairy came running into the garage. The explained that he had received a phone call that there was a bomb in the dairy. He had tried to phone the police, but could not get through. I ran to the phone in the office and rang the police. I told them about the bomb phone call. I give the details where it was at, and told the police we would block traffic from passing the dairy, until they arrived, and hung up.

I told the security man to go back, and block traffic at the junction of Foyle Road, Bishop Street directions. I would block traffic at the junction of Letterkenny Road and Lone Moor Road. Shortly after this, the police and army arrived, with a bomb squad.

They set up the roadblock, and I went back to check the station. After about twenty minutes a land rover pulled into the garage, and a soldier stepped out.

'Are you the person who phoned the police about the bomb?' he asked.

I said, 'Yes I did.'

'We need you to come with us to the barracks for questioning,' he replied.

'What questions?' I said. 'I'm working, I can answer them here.'

'You have to come with us,' he replied.

'Okay, but I need to lock the garage,' I said.

I locked up, and we headed over Foyle Road. The old house on Foyle Road had been demolished, and it was just waste ground now. The driver drove across the waste ground, until he passed the dairy. Suddenly as we pulled back on to the Foyle Road, there was this volley of gunfire.

The driver let out a roar, 'They're shooting at us.'

He pulled back on to the waste ground, and stopped at the back of the Old Star Factory.

The soldier in charge asked me, 'Do you want to get out here?'

I looked at him, 'Are you fucking mental? Take me to the barracks, as quick as possible. Don't you guys get it, anyone seen getting out of a land rover, may as well hang a sign around their neck – Informer.'

The shooting had ceased, and we made it to Victoria Barracks on the Strand Road.

As I stepped out of the land rover I breathed a sigh of relief, just to have got there. Little did I realise then, what I was about to go through.

The barracks were at the back of the police station. In the yard there were about twenty wooden huts in a row. They were about seven feet high and about three feet wide. There were about ten civilians standing in the huts, and it appeared that they were being questioned, as each had a soldier with a gun, talking to them.

I was taken to the hut beside the last in the row, and told to face into the hut, someone would come and question me. As I was standing waiting, I could hear some shouting and arguing from some of the other huts. I started to get a bit nervous. Just then I heard the soldier next at the hut to me, ask the man in the hut, for his name and address. The man gave it and I knew him. He lived in Bluebell Hill Gardens, on Brandywell Road. I peeped in to his hut, and it was him.

'What were you doing when you were arrested?' he asked Danny.

'I was painting the outside of a house,' Danny replied.

'You're a liar, you're a terrorist, and that's not your real name or address.'

Danny turned to face him, 'I'm no terrorist, that's my real name and address. I have never broken the law in my life.'

Danny was now face to face with the soldier.

'Turn around and face the wall,' he shouted at Danny.

As Danny turned round, the soldier struck Danny on the back of his head with the butt of the rifle, and Danny dropped to his knees.

I had seen enough, and I stepped out of the hut, and shouted at the soldier, 'I know this man, he is a neighbour of mine, and I can swear that he is telling you the truth, I won't watch you doing this.'

I can still remember the look on the soldier's face, as we stared at each other, not knowing what would happen next.

He came straight into my face. 'Get back into that hut, before I flatten your face,' he shouted.

I stepped back and replied, 'You lift that gun to hit me, and I swear, that's the last thing you will do today.'

He lifted the rifle above his head, and it was the last thing he did for two hours anyway. As he lifted the gun, I hit him with all I had, and it landed dead on his jawbone, and he fell like a chopped plank, onto his back. I think even Spider Kelly would have been impressed by that punch.

That was the last thing I remembered as well, for an hour at least. After I struck the soldier, a number of soldiers in the line fell to me with rifle butts, and my lights went out.

I woke up later, lying in a large hut. I tried to get up, but felt I was crippled. Every bone and muscle was in pain. There was a soldier standing looking down on me, and when he saw I was awake, he dragged me to my feet. There was a medic soldier sitting at the table. He gave me a quick look over, and said I was fine. I think he studied under Burke and Hare.

I had a pain in my lung, and could hardly breathe, and I was in pain from head to toe. 'Right,' he said, 'sign this and you're free to go.'

I looked at the paper. It was to say I had been questioned, and was not mistreated nor did I see anyone else mistreated while I was there.

'I'm not signing this,' I said.

'If you don't sign it you can go to gaol,' he replied.

'Get the bus, I'm ready for gaol now,' I said. 'I have done nothing only report a phone call about a bomb, stopped traffic so no one would get hurt, agreed to come here to be questioned, and then to defend a neighbour and myself from being assaulted, and you think I will go to gaol?? You won't keep me one day in gaol, you scum.'

I had lost the plot now, for definite, but I just didn't care. The soldier marched me out, and as we crossed the yard, the soldier had to hold me up. The gate opened and a land rover was coming in, and as it did, a local councillor saw me getting dragged across the yard. Liam immediately went to a phone box, and phoned my doctor. The soldier took me to another hut where there were more civilians seated. It was then they told me, after I hit the soldier, the soldiers fell on me. Later, when I was lying in the hut, the soldier I had hit, came in and had a few slaps at me, while I was out cold. Some of them had witnessed it.

After about thirty minutes, there was a knock at the door, and it was my doctor, and he insisted that he would be allowed to examine me, as my doctor. The soldier tried to object, but Dr Fallon was adamant about his rights as my doctor.

They led us into a small room and left us. Dr Fallon gave me a good going over, and was sure that I would be well, after a week's rest.

'Now, Joe,' he said, 'I'm going to tell them that your lung may be punctured, and I need to take you to hospital. That will get you out to get home.'

As soon as I got out of the barracks door, I went to the police station, and reported that I was taking action for assault against a soldier of the Green Howard Regiment. I was told to come back in a day or two. I asked them to take photos of my injuries, and they agreed.

Two days later I went back to the police, and made a statement. My witnesses also made statements, about what they had seen. The bruising was very clear on my body parts now, and there were quite a number. I left the station, and did not really expect to hear much more about the case.

Five months later, the case was called in Derry Courthouse. At the end of the case, the soldier, and his mates, were found guilty of excessive use of force, and the soldier who came and hit me, when I was laying in the hut, was a sergeant, and the judge recommended he should be demoted, and they had to pay me £400 compensation.

I decided after this episode to give up the petrol station work.

Two robberies, bomb scares, fights and a court case, just selling petrol was a bit too much, so I went back to the bar game.

August 1970: A Mix Up of Words

A rare night off for me in months, so I decided I would see if my mate, John McCormick, fancied a night out. We hadn't a night out together in ages, and I missed his company and humour. John and I have been friends since we were kids and still are to this day.

When John was only five, he took tuberculosis and was very ill. He was moved to Musgrave Hospital in Belfast. There they had special treatment wards. These wards were isolated, as were the patients. For parents or family visiting the children, mask and gowns, gloves had to be worn before entry was allowed. The whole world is in the middle of the Covid 19 pandemic as I write this, so I can imagine the scenes in that hospital.

John was one of the very lucky ones, as many children did not survive. Eventually John was fit to be moved back to the St Columb's Hospital in Derry. When he was well on the mend, but still in hospital, we would take him over his clothes, and some we had bought, as he was in hospital for years. Sometimes, we would take him to a dance in the Embassy or Borderland. The nurses knew, but turned a blind eye. John is the kind of friend that everyone should have in their life. The disease left John with a limp in one of his legs, but it never held him back.

We decided we would go to the Collon Bar, at Pennyburn, as John's brother-in-law, Ray Gordon, was playing there. As we were walking down the Strand Road, a foot patrol was coming up. As we passed the foot patrol, one of the soldiers said, 'Alright, mate' to John.

John didn't answer him, as was the done thing then. Next thing we knew we were grabbed by the shoulders and thrown against the Magee College wall.

'Empty your pockets, put your hands against the wall, and spread your legs apart.'

We did what we were told, as this was getting done every day in the town, with all the men. A soldier stepped forward handed his gun to his mate, and began to frisk me down. Then he moved to John, and I started lifting my stuff off the ground.

When he went to frisk John's legs, he kicked his legs further apart. As John had (and still has) a problem standing legs apart, because of the T.B., I roared at the soldier, 'Don't kick him, he has V.D. in the legs.'

The soldier suddenly jumped back from touching John's legs, like he had just been hit by an electric current, and he started to shout, 'Get to fuck, get away from me.'

John lifted his stuff and we walked away. After a few steps we looked back, and the wee soldier was standing, rubbing his hands up and down his trousers, like he was getting rid of some disease.

John and I could not stop laughing. As we walked on, I said to John, 'Sorry about saying that.'

'Don't be sorry, Joe, we have the greatest trick, now, for getting out of searches.' And we had a drink and a laugh about it, and it made the night.

Molin's Club, January 1972: A Town in Shock

I had just returned after a few weeks working in England. I had been working in a pub in Bristol, and it was the wrong time to be working there, considering what was happening here. I hated it and was glad to come home. A friend of mine, who I had worked with in the Roadhouse, Don McLaughlin, was the manager of Molin's Social Club. He offered me a job in the club and I jumped at it.

Molin's Engineering Company was situated in Maydown, and they had their club up in the Beechtree Bar on Beechwood Avenue. The club was well supported by the workers, and a large section of residents from the Rosemount and Creggan areas.

Don and his wife Angela were well known and liked by all in the club. Don was also well respected in the trade, and Angela was a top class Irish dancer, winning many championships. They ran the bar, like a family business.

The club was a great lift after coming home, and the build-up to Christmas created a great atmosphere in the club. Every Sunday the club was packed, as no pubs were allowed to open on a Sunday in the north, but a club was. The weeks flew in to Christmas and the New Year came in with a real great night.

The next big hub of conversation was the approaching big march. As the day grew closer it seemed everyone you spoke to was going on the march. A change was needed by government.

* * *

The day of the march came, and I, like thousands more, went on that march.

That day is well documented on film, pictures, books and newspapers. Like thousands more, I don't need any of these to remind me of that day, or the horror of it. It is replayed in the pictures of my mind forever. The people of Derry were no strangers to marches and riots, but nothing could have prepared them for this.

A few weeks earlier I had been coming down Marlborough Ave on to Marlborough Street from my girlfriend's house. As I crossed the street, shots rang out. I dived down behind a parked car. There was a lookout post the army had in Brooke Park along the wall, facing over Marlborough Street. I thought that a gunman was firing at that, and they were firing back.

It went on for a long time, and I was not for moving, even long after it was over. I was afraid if I went to get up, the lookout post soldiers might have thought it was me who had opened fire, and open fire on me in turn, as it was dark.

I lay there all night till it was bright in the morning. Then I slowly got up, and put my hands above my head, and walked towards the post.

I had only been about thirty yards from the post when the shooting had started, so I knew as soon as I got up from the car, the soldiers could see me. When I got to the post, the soldier shouted down, 'What do you want?'

I told him what happened, and that I had been trapped amid the gunfire. He just shouted down to me, 'Move on, go.' Maybe the suit, shirt and tie said it all.

During the bloodbath on Rossville Street, I had seen soldiers running up the street after the crowd. They were just firing at random, but not for a second did I conceive they were shooting the people dead. Not in cold blood like this. When I got home, my mother had on the news. There were deaths, how many were still not known. I got a cup of tea, then got washed and changed, and headed up to work in the club.

I walked over the Lone Moor Road and up the steps at the bottom of Eastway that lead you up to Beechwood Avenue. I stopped at the top of the steps that overlook the Bogside. My brain could not take it in, people shot dead just a few hours ago. I just started praying for all who were shot, or injured. Then I started up the hill to the club.

As I walked into the club, I could see people in tears, and some just trying to hold it together. It was the worst night you could ever imagine. John Kelly, chairman of the club, had lost his son. Paddy

Duddy who worked in the bar with me, had lost his young brother Jackie. The father of Charlie McGuigan, another lad who served in the bar, had been killed attempting to help a mortally-wounded man. Many of the victim's families attended the club also.

As the night went on, it just got worse No one wanted to leave the club, as every few minutes there were more news reaching us. The media seemed to be very quiet about updates. Looking at the faces of relatives who had lost someone was heartbreaking. Why? For what? All murdered, by the British government's own admission.

After the funerals the club was like the atmosphere of a ghost town. It was awful watching people who had drank, laughed and danced in the club, now just drinking to ease the pain, and cope with their loss.

A few months later I was offered the bar manager job in the Broomhill Hotel, on the Limavady Road. I took the job, but still called up to the club regularly to see my friends.

Broomhill Hotel

1972: LITTLE BIG MAN

I settled in quickly to the Broomhill, and they had a great staff. It was the winter, and the hotel was at the quiet time of the year. It was good for me, as I got a chance to get acquainted with the work. The hotel had a large amount of bookings for weddings from May to September, and a good diary of dinner dances as well. I spoke to John Miskimmon the manager about starting another full time barman. He agreed, and asked me had I anyone in mind. I said, yes, Patsy Loughry. John knew Patsy well. When John worked in the old City Hotel, Patsy was bar manager in the Melville Hotel on Foyle Street. Patsy was a good few years older than me, but I had always admired him, and his style.

Patsy agreed to come and work with me, even though he had given up the bar work a few years earlier. I was just delighted, as I knew Patsy knew all about the hotel game, and every day would be a school day with him.

I didn't have long to wait for my first lesson. Patsy was an instant hit, both with staff and customers. He could talk to people from all walks of life, and they were captured by his good wit and manners. He always came to work in his black dress suit, spotless white shirt and bow tie and, when it came to cleaning the bar, he could roll up his sleeves, and work with the best. Patsy was a real old style barman. Just a real class act.

The usual Saturday afternoon crowd. The City of Derry Rugby team, in for a meal, after they had played their Saturday match. This particular Saturday there were some lads from the local area in for a drink after a football match, they had been at. There was a bit of slagging going on between the two groups, but soon it started to get a bit heated. I told Patsy it was time I stopped this, before it got out of hand.

'Leave it to me,' Patsy replied.

I was not having this, as Patsy would have been sixty by then, five foot four, and about ten stone. Before I could even move, Patsy was out from behind the bar, and in the middle of them, with me beside him.

'Right gentlemen,' he said, 'let's act like men here, and not school kids. Let's show a little respect to one another.'

One football fan tried to push Patsy aside, to continue the row. Suddenly Patsy's two hands were holding his own chest, and he went down on his knees. I just froze, and knew it was a heart attack. Immediately the row was forgot about and, as I knelt beside Patsy, I called for someone to run to reception, and phone an ambulance.

Patsy spoke, 'No, Joe, don't, this has happened before. I will be okay, just get me up sitting in a chair.'

All the lads at the same time went to lift him. We got him on the chair, and give him a sip of brandy. He started to come round. When we were sure Patsy was fine, the football lads left, and the rugby lads went in to the restaurant for their meal.

As the last of them left the bar, Patsy looked at me, with a big smile on his face. 'Works every time Joe,' he said.

I was nearly having a heart attack myself by now. 'Jeepers Patsy,' I said, 'I thought you were dying.'

'Ha, so did they Joe, but when you're a wee man like me, you have to use your brain, when you don't have the brawn.'

Another school day with Patsy.

What a little big man.

Gone now, Patsy, but never forgotten.

1973

I was walking up Rossville Street one night, on my way home after a long day working in the hotel. As I reached Westland Street, I met the famous Mr Paddy (Barman) Duffy. Paddy was a real legend in the town. Professional boxer in his younger days, also an accomplished sketch and oil painting artist. The last forty years, Paddy was the best-known doorman in Derry, and surrounding areas.

He had worked in all the large, well known dance halls: Borderland (Muff), and in Derry at the Corinthian, Guildhall, Embassy, Stardust and many more.

Paddy had seen the boat crews come to Derry from the forties. The

French Canadians, Norwegians, Yanks, British. He had been on the doors when the Joe Loss Orchestra had played in the Guildhall, till Fleetwood Mac, Slim Whitman, and Long John Baldry had played the Embassy in the 1970s. Paddy had seen them all.

'Hello, young Nelis,' he greeted me.

'Hello, Mr Duffy,' I replied.

I had seen Paddy at the door many times at the dances, and had always the greatest respect from him. Never the bully, and had always blessed with loads of common sense. If some lad was refused entry, due to a little too much to drink, and his pals were getting in, Paddy would take the lad aside and suggest he take a little dander in the fresh air for twenty minutes and, Paddy assured him, all would be well, when he returned.

I have never seen it fail.

That was Paddy.

'Just the man I'm looking for, I need a doorman for the Stardust on a Saturday night,' he said, 'and you're the man.'

'Thank you very much for the offer, but I'm not a bouncer,' I said. 'I work in bars, and apart from that Mr Duffy, I can't fight!'

'You won't have to, son,' he said. 'I want someone who can talk to people their own age; I don't want someone who thinks they are Rocky Marciano. You will work at the front door with me, and you have brothers who work there with me, and when it comes to it, they are no slouches, when the going gets a bit tough.'

He assured me I would be fine: 'And it's four pound a night.'

We shook hands and the deal was done. Now I had to get a Saturday night off. This was not going to be easy, as the dinner dances had started in the hotel, every Saturday night.

A few days after my talk with Paddy, I was at work on a Thursday night. There was a good crowd in the bar, mostly business reps, who stayed in the hotel all week, and checked out on a Friday, to go home for the weekend.

Around 8.30pm the manager came running into the bar. John never hurried, so I knew something was badly wrong. He had received a phone call – bomb in the hotel.

'Get everyone out now, Joe.' He was ghostly white.

The alarm bell went off at reception, and it could be heard in Buncrana. We told all the customers to go to the car park on the Limavady Road.

Some of the waiting staff were clearing the restaurant, and kitchen, while other staff were emptying the rooms on the ground level. I told John I would clear the lower rooms, with another member of staff who would guide them up the stairs to the front door exit.

As we were bringing the last of the residents out, I noticed a couple fighting to get back in, but the army, who had arrived, stopped them. They were shouting at the army, but they were Norwegians, and spoke little English.

Suddenly, I remembered earlier that day seeing a small child with them. I called to them I would get the child, by signalling this by rocking my arms, as if holding a baby. I dived back in, down the stairs, to their room. I could hear the baby crying with the alarm sound probably.

In my panic, I had forgotten to get the key for the room. I booted and booted the door, and finally the lock gave way. I grabbed the wee boy from the cot, and ran like a madman up the stairs, and out the front door. I will never forget the look on the parents' faces, as we came through the door, and up through the car park.

The parents had nipped up for a bite to eat in the restaurant, while the baby was fast asleep in the cot. No one expected a bomb scare. Approximately ten minutes later, the bomb went off. It was not a large bomb, but did some damage to a number of rooms, on the same floor that the baby was on.

Later that night, any residents whose rooms were damaged were all moved to the upper floor. All food and drinks the next day were provided free, and residents checking out all received a refund in cash.

John Miskimmon was not one to penny pinch, and always looked after his staff, and customers, always.

Later that day, John called me in to his office. He thanked me for all I had done, and the cool head I had kept. He said, he would like to show his appreciation, as he felt I had saved the hotel from a major disaster, not for saving the hotel, but for the wee boy, and what a loss it would have been.

'Is there anything you would like or need, Joseph?' Never called me Joe.

I explained, I would like a Saturday night off, as I had an offer to work in the Stardust. I said I would enjoy a chance to hear some of the bands as well, as I worked most weekends. I explained that as he was aware of, Patsy never worked nights, but was willing to cover the Saturday nights for me, if John was agreeable. No problem Joseph, I think a few nights out, with a bit of music, just would be a good idea for you, after this, he replied.

John later went to manage the Slieve Donard in Newcastle, County Down.

Another good man. God rest him.

Stardust Dance Hall, 1973

I worked there for several months, doing Saturday nights always. Many class acts appeared there from Joe Dolan to the Drifters to Roy Orbison.

I started off the first few weeks with Barman Duffy, on the front door. Then a new man started, and I was moved upstairs to the dance floor. The doormen worked in twos, and I was paired with my cousin, big Harry Taggart, and I was happy with that.

There were pairs of seats spaced along the dance floor sides, so we could stand on them, and see over the whole dance floor. So if there was trouble in the middle of the dance floor, you could clearly see the doormen on the opposite side, and signal to them to move in.

One night we spotted a fight in the middle of the dance floor. There were maybe six to eight lads involved. I signalled to the doormen opposite, but they were aware of it, and we rushed in. One of the two doormen who came from the opposite side, was my older brother Harry. As we were breaking the fight up, Harry's feet left him, and he landed on his back. As he hit the floor, a guy stepped out from the crowd, and kicked him in the face. We were busy breaking up the fight, but I took a good look at this guy and thought, he will be out the door, as soon as this melee is settled. We got the fighting sorted, and all the doormen marched the guys to the front door. It was an automatic six-month ban for fighting. We went back upstairs to the dance floor. I checked with my brother Harry that he was okay. His eye was beginning to blacken, and the side of his face was swollen. All was quiet the rest of the night. I kept an eye for the guy who had kicked Harry, but no sign of him. I thought maybe he had left with the others.

When the night's music ended, we were redding the hall when I noticed a lad and his girl arguing. As I approached them, he suddenly lifted his fist, and punched her in the face. I was totally shocked. I reached for him and pulled him down the stairs, stood him in front of Barman Duffy at the door. Told Paddy what the guy had done. Paddy just looked at him and spoke: 'Don't come back here, ever, you coward.' Paddy wanted to embarrass him, in front of the crowd round the door, and he did.

I went back up the stairs to check the girl was getting looked after, but she was gone. We cleared the last of the stragglers from the hall down the stairs, and headed down to collect our wages. As we were waiting to get paid, there were three guys standing outside the men's toilets. I recognised the guy who had kicked Harry in the face.

I walked over to where they were, and hit the guy a quick jab on the nose, not enough to do any damage, just enough to cause a bit of a shock, and some pain. His pals just looked shocked.

'It's not very nice to get hit from the blind side, is it?' I said. 'You know now what it feels like. Now get out, and don't come back.'

I walked him over to Barman Duffy, and told him what had happened, and he was barred. Barman caught the guy by the arm and whispered to him: 'You're lucky son, if Harry had got you, you would not be walking home.'

Eventually the place was cleared, and we got paid. I said goodnight to Paddy and the rest of the guys. As I came out the front door, there was a group of girls chatting. As I was passing them, one of the girls came forward to me: 'You're the barman put my fella out, aren't you?'

'Yes,' I said, 'I hope you are not badly hurt.'

She went at me with both hands to my face with her nails, shouting I had no right to interfere in their business, and no right to bar him. It was worse than getting punched in the face, and I could just manage to get away from her. Just one night in the life of a doorman.

Derry City Club, 1974

I left the hotel job at the end of 1973, and took a job in the Derry City Social Club, in Bishop Street. It was originally James & Lowther Laundry, and was a large building. It was now converted into a social club with a large public bar, lounge, snooker and dart room. The Derry City team had pulled out of the Irish League by then, due to the Troubles, which were still serious in the north.

I had been there a few months when the bar manager left for a new job. The club advertised for a new manager, and I applied, and was successful.

The club was well supported, and the players regularly visited the club, but it had been years since the club had been redecorated. I informed the committee I wanted them to agree to close the club for one week. This would give the club a fresh look, and a chance to give it a good cleaning all over. I also wanted a chance to interview some people for staff jobs, as I felt we needed to strengthen the staff we had, and hire a few more staff with experience. Most of the staff employed at the time, were young college boys.

One lad I was set on keeping was a lad called Garvin Kerr. Garvin, for his age was the best young man behind a bar I have ever seen, and more than forty years later, and working with a few hundred bar staff, he is still the best. The committee were not very keen on the changes, but they reluctantly agreed.

I made a phone call to Guinness offices in Belfast, and asked if I could meet with a company executive. I met with two of them a few days later, and explained that, even though the club was doing well, I believed we could become the club with the biggest turnover in Northern Ireland. I felt that they would benefit from the rise in sales. Therefore, I asked them if they would put up half the money for the renovations. I was shocked when a few days later, they phoned me to say, not only were they going to pay for all the renovations, but on our opening night, they were donating five kegs of Stout, Harp and Smithwick's. How things have changed with the drinks companies!

The work was all finished in a week, and the club looked like a new club. Seating all recovered, tables all revarnished and a great paint job all over.

We reopened on a Saturday night, with a new staff, mostly. Garvin and I ran the front bar with two part-timers. In the lounge, behind the bar, was my brother Johnny, who had earlier managed the Roadhouse, and Tommy Carlin, a work colleague in the Post Office, but a natural barman, and again two part-time lads to help them.

The night was a great success, and the Dillon Brothers provided a great night's music.

The weeks that followed proved that the work had paid off.

I raffled a bottle of spirits every Friday, Saturday and Sunday nights, and the profits of the bottles went a good way towards paying staff wages.

Things were going very well, and the committee were very happy with the results.

I always enjoyed, on a quiet night, to try and get a chat to regulars in having a pint, if they had any ideas they would like to suggest, that might improve the club, service, or add something to the facilities we had in the club.

I noticed that one of their regular friends was not in their company that night, and he had not been in for a few weeks. I asked the lads if he was unwell, or had they heard from him.

'It's his wife, Joe,' they told me, 'she is unwell.'

'What's wrong with her?' I enquired.

'She has a brain illness, and it's very serious.'

I went to see him the next day, with two of his pals. He explained to me that his wife had been to hospital and had all the tests and scans done. She needed an operation, but nowhere in Britain had performed this type of operation before. It had been done only in America, with mixed results. This operation was her only chance of recovery. They had discussed it with consultants and family, and were going to fly to America, in hope of success.

That night, I went and spoke to the Secretary of the club, Willie Ross. I told him the situation the family were in and asked him to call a committee meeting the next night. We met the next night, and it was clear that the committee, and staff would raise as much money for the family as possible, through raffles, and donations. We did not have a date, when the lady would travel to America, but we started the ball rolling that night. The main draw would be for a five hundred pounds cash prize. The committee also set up a three-man party, who collected a ledger of private donations. The staff and musicians volunteered part of their wages nightly. The tickets went like wildfire, and I constantly had to run to a shop for more books of tickets. I kept in touch with the family every few days. Then the consultant phoned them from Altnagelvin to say, if the family would come to the hospital in Washington, the hospital would perform the operation, and the aftercare free – if they thought the lady would have a chance of surviving the operation.

The family agreed, and the date they would fly out was made. Now that we had a date, all in the club made a real concerted effort, to get as much money as possible. Even though we were busy in the club, it was constantly in your mind, what the family and the couple were going through.

One of the best memories about selling the tickets was how many people, when buying the tickets, said, 'No, don't put my name on the tickets Joe, put the family's name on it.'

I thought it was a lovely idea. This idea was soon followed by many people. The draw was to take place a few days before the family were due to fly off.

I asked Willie Ross if he would like to make the draw. Willie said he had a man in mind, a well-respected, long-time Derry City supporter, who had followed the team through thick and thin. It would be nice to ask him.

The next day, I called to the man's house and asked if he would do the draw for us. He was delighted. He then said to me, 'Joe I want to talk to you seriously, have you time for a cuppa?'

I said, 'Of course, I'm all ears.'

I thought it was about one of his stories, about bother at a match, or something like that. He loved telling old stories, but it was far from that. Which I shall come back to later.

The night of the draw came, and the club was jammed. Tickets were still being sold and donations offered. At nine o'clock, all the tickets were emptied into a big metal drum, and they were given a good burl round. The elderly man stepped forward, and a loud round of applause for him ensued. The place went silent, and the lady's family were sitting at the first table. As the draw began, the gentleman put his hand into the drum, swirled his hand round a few times, then picked out a ticket. He looked at the number 904, silence, then he turned the ticket over, to see the name on the back. He looked totally shocked, as if he had picked out his own ticket.

He turned and looked at the crowd, 'Folks, you won't believe this,' he said, as a few called up, 'Not you yourself?'

'No,' he said, 'even better.'

And he held up the ticket for us to see. It belonged to the family whose mother was ill. The place exploded, with cheers, applause, women and men were crying. I have never heard euphoria like that night, and never since. The cheering just went on and on, while the family, getting hugs from everyone, just wanted to let their mother and father hear the news.

The lady and the family flew out a few days later, with the prayers, and good wishes from everyone. We received a phone call to the club about a week later, operation successful, and recovery going well. Hope to be home in a couple of weeks. They did arrive home almost three weeks later, and the lady made a full recovery.

And now for the footnote…

After I had asked the gentleman to do the draw a few days before the big night, we started talking about the family, and the expense of flying to America. If all went well, how long would the family need to stay there? Secondly, what if it doesn't?

'I don't want to think about that,' I said.

'The family will think about it, Joe,' he replied, 'they have to.'

'What are you trying to tell me?' I said.

'Well, Joe,' he started again, 'be honest with yourself, who needs money more than this family now? They have enough to worry about now, God knows.'

He looked at me, and I could see the seriousness in his face.

'Don't be naïve Joe, do you think people bought these tickets to win? he continued. 'No way, they wanted to help this family, and that is the right thing to do, Joe.'

So we rigged the draw. That was forty-six years ago.

I met him a few years later, and we had a chat. 'Tell me, Joe, do you regret what we did?'

'No,' I said, 'not for a single second.'

'Nor I,' he replied.

We left it at that!

The Catholic Club

1974: SWITCHING CLUBS

As the year was coming to the end, there was talk that the club and surrounding houses were being demolished for a new housing scheme. Lots of old houses in the area, and different areas in the town were being demolished and new houses were being built.

I received a visit one night at home, from a member of the Catholic Club Committee. He explained that the manager of the club was retiring, and asked would I consider taking over the job. The salary was better, shorter hours and there was a free flat for accommodation, if I needed it. I was already engaged to be married the following year, and a free flat was a real bonus. I talked to my girlfriend, and we thought it would be a good move.

I handed in my two-week notice, and started in the Catholic Club, after a week's break.

It was a big change from the Derry City Club. No music, and no ladies allowed. It was simply a man's club. There was a huge, seated barroom on the second floor, a television/reading room on the third, and a snooker room on the ground floor. The flat was on the top floor. It was mostly made up of members who had good jobs, businessmen and clergy.

A non-member could only be signed in by a member, if the non-member lived fifteen miles outside of Derry. A Protestant could be signed in from anywhere, but could not become a member. They were very strict about the rules.

The club was run in a very Dickensian style, with no laughter or craic.

1975

The club opened from twelve noon till 2.00pm and from 7.00pm until midnight daily.

It was there that I first met Newell McBride. Newell worked as a compositor, with the Derry Journal, and worked part time a few nights a week in the club. I liked Newell instantly; straight talking with a great dry wit.

Little did I have a clue that night I met him that our friendship, and working together would last over the next forty years.

Newell was one of the best men you could ever work with. Honest, hardworking, thoughtful, and just as dependable, but never afraid to give his opinion, on any subject when asked. I really looked forward to the nights we were working together. You were always sure of a laugh when Newell was working.

I remember a cold winter's night in February, I had lit the open fire in the TV room, as some members would go up to watch the nine o'clock news.

I was called to the TV room to bring a round of drinks. There was a bishop, two priests, a Protestant minister and two well-dressed businessmen. Newell arrived up with a coalscuttle to top up the fire. When he saw them all sitting round the fire, he smiled at me: 'This is what hell will look like, Joe – you won't see the fire, for the white collars round it. The bishop and ministers all laughed heartily, but for some reason the businessmen did not find it so funny.

The club was a very different kind of job to what I had been used to. During the day, a few members may have called in for a game of snooker at lunchtime, or to have a read of the daily papers. They seldom had a drink, but I still had to be available. The days were spent mostly cleaning. At night there could be ten or twenty customers, and it was usually the same faces. They sat usually in groups of three or four at a table, and usually in the same company. There was no craic, and not even any conversation, between the barman and the members. It was always hushed conversations. I missed the music, and the banter with customers.

One of the few occasions, Newell and I got a real laugh. The two of us were behind the bar, when a local doctor called in for a drink. He had had a long day, and was glad to get finished. He had finished late and left his car at home, and walked down to the club, for a nightcap. Newell put him up a Power's whiskey with ice and ginger ale. Just then the phone rang, and I answered it.

'Hello, is that the Catholic Club?' a lady's voice spoke.

'It is, can I help you?' I replied.

'Is Doctor so-and-so there, please? I need to speak with him.'

'I will check for you, Ma'am, what's the name please?'

She gave her name. I told the doctor about the call, and he spoke to her. When he had finished, he asked me to ring him a taxi, to bring his bag up to him and then take him to Shantallow. The taxi came in a few minutes, and the doctor told me to hold his drink.

'I won't be long Joe,' he said, and he left.

Less than an hour later, the doc returned. I got him a fresh drink, and asked if he was sorted. I'm fine Joe, just a mother worried about nothing. As he stood at the bar, with Newell and I, he took a drink of the whiskey, and smiled.

'What?' Newell asked.

'It was a wee boy about five, and his wee penis was stiff for two days, and his mother was panicking,' he explained.

He told the mother it was caused by a muscle spasm, which would relax naturally, and would do the boy no harm. As the doc got up to leave the house, he lifted his bag and was leaving, as the taxi was waiting for him.

'Are you not going to give him anything for it doctor?' the woman asked.

The doctor turned and answered, 'I would give half my surgery for it, Ma'am.' And left.

I would love to have seen the woman's face. A bit of banter for one night in the club.

That September, after a honeymoon in Spain, my wife and I moved into the flat. We were both working full time. And at the weekends, we did not get much time together as I worked Saturday and Sundays, and had only one night a week off.

Even though we lived in the club, my wife could not even come down to the bar to speak to me, as there were no ladies allowed in the club. By November, I had made up my mind to look for another job.

I carried on as normal for the next few weeks. Shortly after the beginning of the New Year, Newell came to see me one afternoon.

There was a new pub opened in Butcher Street, The Gate Inn. Newell knew the owner well, and he told Newell he was looking for a manager.

Newell recommended me, and I knew the owner, as Shaun had owned the Stardust when I had done doorman a few years earlier. I met Shaun a week later, and he told me he would be happy if I would consider the job. I told him I would speak to my wife, and check if she was happy with the move.

It was better money, plus a flat, more time off, so we both agreed to the move. A few days later, I asked Newell, would he leave the part-time job at the club, and work part-time in the bar. I explained to him I could choose my own staff. Newell went one better; he gave up the Journal, and started with me, full-time. I was delighted, and we could not wait to get started.

The bar was beautifully decorated, in light and dark greens, with polished mahogany tables. The bar behind was a very modern layout. Upstairs there was a lounge/dining room, with a small bar. Also a good well-fitted kitchen. Again our flat was on the top floor. The flat was well furnished, with television, radio, phone, and also a good size kitchen, and bedroom. We were both very happy with the move, and Newell being with us was the cream on the cake.

The Gate Inn

1976: A NEW BEGINNING

Newell and I started the first day together, and for me it was great, getting back to the kind of bar I loved. Situated in the town centre, with a good passing trade, and food available from midday to 4.00pm daily. On Saturdays it was available from midday to 6.00pm. We also catered for private parties upstairs at night. Getting the Sundays off was a real bonus. Betty and Lily looked after the cooking and cleaning. Great workers, and the food was first class. The whole staff gelled really well. Within a few weeks we were doing a great deal of business, and the takings showed it as the weeks passed.

Huntwright's Factory was just round the corner, on Magazine Street, and the workers there often came in for their lunch breaks. The shops and office workers in the area supported the bar daily and, at night, after they finished work, some would call in for a drink on their way home. This was on top of the daily passing trade, people going to the town, or shoppers on their way back home.

Newell had always wanted to learn how to make some cocktails, but there hadn't been much point, when we were in the club working. So after we finished in the Gate at night, I showed him how to make a half-a-dozen different cocktails. From Dressed Pimm's to Brandy Alexander. He took to it like a duck to water. After a couple of weeks, he suggested we should put them on, as a special on a Saturday. They went a bomb with the ladies.

I don't know to be honest, if it was the drinks, or if they just loved the look of the glasses, with the fruit and umbrellas, with the lit sparkler and the straw. Newell was in his element on a Saturday, as more and more women would call in for a cocktail, after their shopping was done, or when heading home after work. He was Derry's Tom Cruise in the Cocktail film, at the time.

Opposite the bar was Deery's Music Shop. Musicians would call in there to buy instruments or maybe just a set of new strings for a guitar or a banjo. Sometimes they would come across to the bar for a pint and to restring their instruments. Many a good session we enjoyed, with someone starting a song on his guitar and being joined by other musicians.

Usually, on a Saturday night when we were closed and the bar tidied, we would have a staff drink before we went home. Newell would praise how good Lily and Betty were at their jobs, and then he would turn to me, and just loud enough for them to hear, he would say to me, when are we going to get some decent workers in here. It was just a great bit of craic to finish the week. Bar work is just like life. Nothing stays great forever, and neither does it stay terrible.

The blips are never far away in the bar game. The next was closer than I imagined, and a bit more than a blip.

1976: SUMMER

It was the summer of 1976. A beautiful summer day. It was my lunch hour, and I wanted to go for a walk round the town, and get a bit of the sun. I told Newell I would be back in an hour, and let him go for his lunch.

I was walking back toward Ferryquay Street towards the Diamond, after my walk, when I noticed a crowd starting to gather at the Diamond. As I got to the Diamond I could hear people mumbling about a bomb somewhere. I looked across at Butcher Street and it was being cordoned off. Suddenly Newell and the rest of the staff were beside me.

'Jesus Joe, there's a bomb in the bar, and one in Deery's Music Shop.'

I could hardly take in what he was saying. My first thought was, thank God, my wife is at work, and we had no children to worry about.

I asked Newell if the bar was definitely empty, and were Deery's staff and customers all out for sure. He assured me the army had received the call about the bomb, and they had received the code word with it. So they immediately had cleared the entire street, and businesses and offices. After a few minutes I had taken it all in. Suddenly there was a large explosion. It came like a wartime scene, as the dust came along the street, like a storm. A minute later another explosion, it was Deery's. The bar and Deery's wiped out in a few minutes. For a few minutes after the second bomb, nobody moved, like we were waiting for another bomb. The crowd started chatting after a few minutes, and began moving away.

As I stood there I began to think about the damage to the bar, but thank God, nobody was injured. The building could be fixed, lives can't. Sometime later, the all clear was given. The staff from Deery's and ourselves walked down to inspect the damage.

The bar was destroyed, and the two first floors had collapsed into the cellar. Only the floor of my flat, on the top storey, was left there. Deery's was completely demolished. As we stood looking into the rubble there were parts of guitars and drums, lying in there, which had been blown across the street, and in Deery's, there were chairs and stools from the bar. As I looked up at where our flat was, I realised that all our wedding presents were all ruined now. The only thing I could see was our double bed, which was a wedding gift, from my wife's mum and dad. I decided, there and then, I would get it out.

I rang Shaun the owner of the bar, and told him what had happened. We arranged to meet the next morning at 9.00am. I then rang a construction company, and hired a crane and driver to meet me at 7.00am the next day.

I told the staff I would speak to Shaun in the morning, but it looked like we were all unemployed.

The next morning at 7.00am, the crane and driver were at the bar.

'Right, how do you want to do this?' the driver asked.

'I want you to strap me in and lift me onto the top floor,' I said.

'If you show me how to connect the straps to the four corners of the bed, then I will sit on the bed, then you can bring us down together.'

'Right, no problem,' he said, but the look on his face was clear. He thought I was nuts.

He showed me how to secure the straps to the bed, securely and balanced. Then he secured the straps around me. He got back into the crane, and I began to go up. As I got higher and started to swing a little, I was glad it was him who tied the straps. My heart was beating a little faster now. The driver was very careful, and in no time at all, I was above the bed.

Very slowly he lowered me onto the bed. I sat for a minute to gather myself. Then I started to release the straps from me, and tie them to the corners, moving very, very slowly. As I tied the last corner of the bed, I noticed he had an extra strap which still secured me to the crane. I gave him the thumbs up, and the bed lifted slightly, and then touched the floor again. Again the bed began to rise, and as it did, the floor beneath us collapsed, straight down onto the rubble below. I was shaking, but held on for dear life to the strap. When I was back on the ground, and the driver had released me, my legs were so weak, I could hardly get off the bed.

Unbelievably the bed was not damaged; there was nothing else left in the flat. The crane driver left, with a good tip for his common sense and, shortly after that, a friend came with a van to remove the bed.

I met Shaun the owner, as planned, at 9.00am. There was nothing he could do, so we shook hands and he wished me the best of luck, as I did him. That afternoon I met the staff and told them how sorry I was that we would have to look for a job, but wanted to meet up and have a last drink together.

Newell had already been contacted by the boss of the Journal, as he had heard about the bomb, and offered Newell his old job back at the newspaper. I was delighted, as he had a family to support.

When I got home to my mother's house, where we were now staying, my mother told me, that afternoon, a man had called to see me. He owned the Park Bar, and was looking for a manager. I went to see Christy, the next day, which was a Sunday, and the day after that, I started as manager of the Park Bar in Francis Street.

The Park Bar, 1976

When I started in the Park Bar, I was pleasantly surprised at the number of customers I had known over the years. One in particular was my cousin, Harry Taggart; he and I had worked a few years earlier together, as doormen in the Stardust.

There were a number of great characters in the bar. The regulars were a great bunch of people, some still drink there, and sadly some have passed away, but are still remembered, by their stories, and friends. As soon as I got the first couple of weeks over, and started to enjoy the craic and the atmosphere of the bar, I knew Newell would enjoy working here. Newell only lived up the street from the bar, and he called in to wish me good luck. I asked him if he would do some part time for me, and he was delighted to be back working in a bar again, and he knew a lot of the regulars as well.

Saturday morning, my favourite day of the week in a bar. Racing and football on the television, and all the regulars in for the day's craic, after a week's work. My cousin Harry always came early on a Saturday morning, to help get the bar ready, and open up. I opened the door at 11.00am, and put Harry a bottle of stout. As I was pouring Harry's stout, an elderly man walked into the bar. We had never seen him before – a complete stranger.

'Good morning, what can I get you?' I asked.

'Can I have a half of Jameson please?' he replied.

'Certainly sir,' and I poured the whiskey. 'Would you like some water with it?'

'Yes please,' he answered.

As I handed him the jug of water, he commented, 'I'm just thinking son, it's a bit early in the day to be drinking whiskey, could I have a bottle of Guinness instead?'

'No problem,' I said, as he had not touched the whiskey.

I poured his stout into a glass, and he took a drink of it.

'Lovely,' he said.

I lifted the whiskey glass and took the whiskey bottle down off the showcase. I took the optic off the bottle, and poured the whiskey back into the bottle, and replaced the bottle back on the showcase. I turned back to the man, and his glass was empty of the stout, and he was walking towards the door.

'Excuse me sir, you didn't pay me for the stout.' I smiled as I spoke.

'I gave you a whiskey for it', he replied.

'You didn't pay me for the whiskey,' I said.

'I didn't drink the whiskey,' he replied, as he walked out the front door.

Caught by an old gentleman, with a real con job! Harry was in stitches, when I looked at him. Caught for twenty-eight pence, but a lesson I never forgot. What could I do? I was not going to pull him at his age, back into the bar, for the price of a stout.

Harry said, 'He probably spends the day pulling that trick in every bar he visits.'

'Good luck to him Harry,' I said.

Years later, I still call into the Park Bar for a drink. John White is the manager now, and is an absolute gentleman and first class barman.

* * *

One day this young red-haired lad walked into the bar, and enquired if there were any jobs available. He was very shy, but something about the lad was likable instantly. His name was Martin Ferguson. His dad drank in the bar, and I knew most of his family.

'Why do you want to work in a bar?' I asked.

He thought for a moment, and then replied: 'I just like people.' The best answer he could have given, for me. Anyone can learn to work in a bar but, to be good at it, you have to like people.

I stayed there for two years, before moving to the Alleyman's Bar on the Strand Road.

Martin stayed in the Park, and later he moved to Tinney's Bar, in Patrick Street.

Later Martin became manager of the bar for years. He was one of the hardest working lads I have ever worked with, and as honest as a day's long. Later we were to meet up again, doing the doorman's work at the Venue, and the Post Office Club. Martin's family were all grafters, so it was no surprise, when Martin was the same.

In 1978, Mickey Owens, the manager of the Alleyman's Bar on the Strand Road was leaving to open up his own butcher shop.

I was asked if I would be interested in a move to the Alleyman's. The wages were better, and as we had bought our first house, the money was a big factor in my decision to take the job.

The Alleyman's Bar, 1978

The Alleyman's, much like the Park Bar, had its own characters, from Mickey (Shannon) Gallagher the professional wrestler, to Mickey Nicell the singer and great story teller, to Piercy Anderson.

Piercy was the man. He worked in the hospital full time. Piercy sold the raffle tickets, for the weekly draw, ran the dart competitions and if you wanted a bet done in the bookie's shop down the street, Piercy was your man. Piercy was like everyone's da. I was only there a couple of weeks and there was an argument between Piercy and a guy, much younger than Piercy. I came out from behind the bar, to end it, as it was getting near coming to blows. I got in between them and told them to calm down, as the younger guy was threatening to hit Piercy.

'Come on,' I said, 'have a bit of respect for an older man.'

Piercy turned and looked at me, like I was mad.

'Do you know your problem Joe?' he said, as he pointed his finger to the tip of his nose. Everyone just laughed and it was all over. That was Piercy.

On another occasion, Mickey Owens, the previous manager, who just lived up the street, was not well. When he was on the mend, Piercy and I called in to visit him. Piercy had just finished work and was in for a pint. I asked him to go up to see Mickey. While we were up with Mickey, his sister brought us some tea. Mickey hadn't eaten anything for a couple of days. Piercy said he had some lovely salmon sandwiches left over from the lunch pack his wife had made earlier that day. Mickey said he would try one. As Mickey tucked into the sandwich and tea, I asked Piercy how was work that day.

'Just another day, Joe, except I had to help out at the morgue today. An old man died and I had to wash him down. I thought I would have to use a hose on him, he was filthy.'

I looked at Mickey's face, and he had stopped chewing. He was just holding the sandwich up to his face, and staring at it. Mickey took an extra week to recover.

Like most local bars, the regular bars, the regular men folk would spend a few hours on a Saturday afternoon having a few drinks, and watching the racing. Then head home around five, get their dinner and most of them would be back at nine, with their mates, wives or girlfriends. There was always music in the upstairs lounge, on a Saturday night. We always had a pot of stew ready in the bar on a Saturday, just to keep everybody happy, and fed.

One of our regulars drove a steamroller for the city council, as his full time job. This particular Saturday, he had to work, and he was not happy about it, as a Saturday was his big day out. He parked the roller on the street behind the bar, so if anyone from the council passed the bar, it would not be spotted. He came into the bar and asked for a big plate of stew, and a pint. He banged the roller keys down on the counter, and started to tell me, he was not a bit pleased about having to work on a Saturday. Two lads going down to put on a bet in the bookies asked him if he wanted any bets placed. He picked out a couple of horse bets, and he wrote them down. He handed them the bets and the cash, and away they went.

After they returned and gave him his receipts, he left. Five minutes later he was back.

He was shouting all over the bar. 'Somebody stole the steamroller Joe, they have hijacked it!'

Somebody shouted out, 'The cops will have their work cut out, catching it!' Roars of laughter.

The driver was shouting. 'But I have the keys, how are they driving it?'

Just then another lad came into the bar, and heard all the fuss. 'It's sitting up in College Square,' he said.

The driver was out the door like a shot. It took him a long time to work it out. The two lads, who took his bet, lifted his keys while he was writing his bet, and sat them back on the counter when they were giving him the receipt. He never worked a Saturday ever after that.

* * *

On a Saturday night, Piercy ran a dart competition for two sirloin steaks. The winner had two steaks for the Sunday dinner, and bragging rights for the week in the bar. The dart finished around nine, and then most would head upstairs for the music.

At around 8.45pm, the final of the darts was about to begin, and there was a good crowd already in the lounge. Just then the phone in the bar rang.

I answered it, 'Hello, Alleyman's Bar.'

'Who is this speaking?' the voice asked.

'It's Joe, the manager, who is speaking?'

The voice came back. 'Listen carefully,' he said. 'This is the IRA there's a bomb planted in the bar, you have fifteen minutes to get everyone out. You got that, fifteen minutes, this is not a hoax.'

I told my downstairs colleague, Charlie Marley, to go upstairs and tell Garvin Kerr, the other barman, to redd the lounge, and get them down to the Strand Road, and phoned the police. After we had emptied the bar and the lounge, some of our regulars knocked on doors, close to the bar, to let them know. There were also houses at the back of the bar, Rock Terrace, and we let them know as well. Then the police and army arrived, and took over. The traffic was all blocked off from passing the bar, and the crowd were all a safe distance away.

Then we just waited, and waited, and the thoughts of the bomb in Broomhill Hotel came back to me. If a bomb went off in the bar, it would wreck houses and shops nearby as well. Still we waited. After what seemed like an hour, an army officer came and spoke to me.

'We believe it's a hoax call,' he said.

'What do we do now?' I asked.

'Well we need to send in an explosives officer, to check the building, before we can give you the all clear,' he said. 'There could be a hoax bomb in the building, so we need to check the whole inside.'

Just then a soldier came forward and asked me the layout of the bar. He had on like a heavy metal jacket, and he looked no more than twenty years old.

I said to the officer in charge, 'He looks very young.'

'He's all we have,' he said. 'It's been a bad week in Belfast for bombs, and most are up there. As soon as we get the all clear, you can let the customers back in to the bar.'

'Listen,' I said, 'I know every inch of that bar, lounge, and cellar. All the seats in the lounge are built in seating, and they all lift up, anything could be planted there. If he misses anything, these people will be killed, and the houses around here will be wrecked. I'm going in with him.'

'Are you mad?' the officer said. 'I can't let you do that.'

'If you want that lad of yours to have a chance to get out of that bar, I'm your best chance, and I am going in with him.'

So, we went in together; first the bar and toilets. Then the cellar, all good so far, but truth be told, I was shaking. Then up to the lounge. First, as we went into the lounge was the toilets, all clear. Now just the lounge, checked behind the lounge bar, nothing there, then seat by seat, lifting the bottoms up and checking underneath. Once we locked eyes, and to tell the truth, he looked scared stiff, and he probably saw that I looked the same.

As we walked down the alleyway steps, back to the Strand Road, my legs were like water jelly.

We crossed the street to where the army were.

'All clear,' he said to the officer.

Then he turned to me, and in a very quiet voice, said, 'Thank you, thank you so much.'

'No,' I said, 'thank you.' I said, and we shook hands.

The army then removed the traffic barriers, and the traffic started moving. I said to the customers, we should call it a night, but they were not having it. So we went back in for last drinks.

While I was serving last drinks, Andy came up to me, and I got what winning the steaks meant to some dart players.

'Joe,' he said, 'will you give the two steaks to Jim?'

Jim was the other finalist along with Andy.

'Why?' I said, 'we could play the final now, before we go.'

'No, Joe, when you were redding the bar out, Jim asked me if I wanted to play one leg of darts for the final winner of the steaks. I said, no Jim, you're welcome to them.'

High steaks indeed.

* * *

One of my favourite customers ever to come into the bar was the late Claude Wilton. Famous Derry solicitor, a great wit, and a true gentleman. If you were going to court, and you knew you stood little chance, you went to Claude. He was the working man's hero. Even the judges loved him.

I remember well one Friday night, a regular and good friend of Claude's came into the bar for his usual pre-weekend drinks.

'Is Claude in yet Joe?' he asked.

'Not yet, but he will probably show up soon,' I replied.

Claude always called in on a Friday night, and he always ended up with an audience, with his witty stories.

'Is everything alright?' I asked him.

'No, Joe, my son took his car out last night and had a few drinks, then some of his friends wanted to go to a dance in Letterkenny. While driving up the road, he hit some bollards in the middle of the road. The Guards were there, and they arrested and charged him with driving while drunk. He's up in court next week in Letterkenny.'

Just then, in walks Claude. The regular called for a drink for both of them, and he started to tell Claude the story. When he had finished, Claude asked him, what was the alcohol reading.

'It was 200-and-something per 80 millilitres of blood,' he replied. 'Right, I will represent him next week. And tell him not to worry, I hear Portlaoise Gaol is all done up now – it's lovely!' And Claude just chuckled, as he looked at his friend.

There are many stories about Claude, some true, and some made up, but my favourite of them all, was the one he told me out of his own mouth. A guy once came to him and said he was arrested at home on a Saturday night, just as he was ready to go for a drink.

A jewellery shop owner in the town said that around 3.30pm on that Saturday, a man had run into the shop, grabbed some necklaces and some gents' watches, that had been on show on the counter, and had run out of the shop, before anyone could stop him. A lady coming into the shop, knew the thief, and was able to identify him; she even gave the police his name.

When he told Claude the story, Claude said to him, 'But aren't you always at the Derry City matches on a Saturday afternoon?'

The man looked at Claude in a quizzical way. 'Oh yes, yes, Claude, I was at the match from three o'clock to five.'

'Well, you couldn't have robbed the shop at three-thirty then, could you? Now what you need to do is to get as many of your friends who were at the match, to come as witnesses for you.'

The man was beaming, 'Right Claude.'

The day of the trial, the defendant turned up with over forty witnesses. The judge heard the first part of the case, and the lady witness's testimony. The judge knew that the rest of the week would be taken up by Claude calling these witnesses one by one to testify that they had been with the defendant, at the match. The judge ended it very quickly, by thanking the lady for her help, but in this case, it was clearly a case of mistaken identity. There was a round of applause from all his friends, as the defendant was told he was free to go.

As Claude and the defendant were going out of the court, the defendant asked Claude for his fee. 'Don't worry, it's fine, you can get me a drink some time.'

The defendant was adamant that he would give something for Claude's time.

'Okay,' said Claude, 'I'll take one of them watches.'

'The man had a serious drink problem Joe, and it was done for drink in desperation. I knew him well Joe, and I knew he was harmless.'

Claude went back that night to see him, and he still had the stuff, and he asked if there was any way he could give it back, without anyone knowing. Claude took the stuff, and it was returned by post, to the jeweller a few days later. Is it any wonder the whole town loved Claude? As the local law motto reads: 'Say nothing till you see Claude.'

Scottish and Newcastle, 1979

Around the end of 1979, the Scottish and Newcastle rep called in for his order. Eamon Gallagher had been their salesman for twenty years in the Northwest, and before that, he was the salesman for J. & T. McGinley's Tea, for over thirty years. I had been friends with Eamon for years, and he was a real character. Loved his game of bridge, with a gin and tonic, and was the king of one-liners. He was telling me that he was going to retire at the end of the month.

'I think you should apply for the job, Joe,' he said.

I was really flattered by this, as Eamon knew his stuff, and was not the kind of man to puff you up.

'I don't know Eamon, I've never done sales before.'

'You're selling everyday Joe, it's just you're selling to the owner, instead of your customers. No difference. I have mentioned your name, to my boss, Joe. It's a good job, with a good salary and car.

Then he mentioned another barman in the town, who had known Eamon was leaving, and was applying for the job.

'What's his chances?' I asked Eamon.

'I could learn to live without him,' he smiled, and that was it.

I gave Eamon my order, and he left. The following week, there was an advert in the paper for the job. I applied that day, and got a reply, to attend an interview in the Everglades Hotel. I went for the interview, and there were about fifteen to twenty others there, waiting as well.

When I was finally called in and gave them my history so far, they explained about the job. The man doing the interviews was called Des Dixon, director of the firm, and head of the Northern Ireland Distribution.

'Well, Mr Nelis, we have one hundred and thirty applicants to interview over the next few days. Why do you think I should pick you for the job?'

I knew, this was the part, where my answer would determine whether I was in or out.

'Well, Mr Dixon, I know almost every bar owner, and manager in this town, and many outside. I have a good relationship with them all. I work hard, and I understand most of the problems that bars face. I have no problems working long hours or spending nights at special functions, to promote our products, on these nights. Lastly Mr Dixon, I believe that I am honestly, the best man for this job, and I believe if you don't pick me, you could have sleepless nights, as the sales could easily drop in the Northwest, after Eamon leaves. I believe Guinness will make a big effort to win over your customers, as a lot of them bought the orders because of their esteem they held for Eamon.'

'Thank you Mr Nelis, you will receive word in a few days, if you are shortlisted, if you are not shortlisted, thank you for your time,' he finished.

'Thank you for yours too,' I replied.

Two days later I received a phone call at home.

'Is that you Mr Nelis?'

'Yes,' I replied.

'This is Des Dixon calling, just to let you know you got the job. Can you start two weeks from Monday?'

He was very upbeat in his voice.

'Sure I can, but what about the shortlist?' I said.

'Forget about that, I don't want any sleepless nights, see you up on the Newtownards Road in Belfast in two weeks. Bye.'

I immediately rang Eamon, to tell him my good news.

'I know, Joe,' he laughed, 'and I have arranged to take you round the first week and introduce you to everyone.'

I thanked Eamon, and hung up, Being on the road with Eamon, was going to be a real eye-opener.

I started my first week on the job, with Eamon keeping me right, after a meeting on the Monday with Mr Dixon. Eamon was a joy to travel with, and a lifetime of stories in the sales game. Eamon spoke very proper, and could deliver a story like no other.

One of his favourites was when he went into one of his usual customers for an order. The bar owner said that a lady had complained that the new brand of gin Eamon had sold him was not good and did not taste right.

'What did she drink with the gin?' Eamon asked him.

'Tonic water, she always takes it with tonic water.'

Eamon asked him to put up two gins, and one tonic water. Eamon sipped the first gin, then poured some tonic into the second gin, and sipped it. Then he took a sip of the tonic water, straight from the bottle, and made a terrible face.

'There's your problem, the tonic is off.'

He told me: 'The best of all Joe, he never questioned it, and never mentioned it again, but still bought the old cheap gin.'

As we visited each pub, Eamon introduced me, and asked each in turn that he hoped they would support me, as I was a straight salesman and that he had recommended me for the job. When I lifted Eamon one morning, he informed me that a publican he had been friends with for years had passed away, after a long illness. We were going to the funeral later that morning.

As we were at the graveside, and the coffin was being slid from the back of the hearse, and just as the coffin bearers were holding the coffin, suddenly there was a crack, and the remains fell out of the bottom of the coffin. The full bottom of the coffin just collapsed. It was truly awful to see. For the family and friends, it was horrific. I could not believe what I was witnessing, and I was just an onlooker. Another coffin arrived, and after the prayers were finished, and the funeral over, Eamon spoke to the family.

The family had paid for an expensive coffin for their father, and felt they had not gotten the quality they had paid for. Two weeks later the firm of undertakers was up for sale in a number of papers. Exactly what Eamon's first words to me, as we got into the car, the day of the funeral. 'That's that firm finished Joe, no mistake.'

For the next year, I worked hard at building up my sales, and was doing well. At some of the monthly meetings Des made it clear that sales were slowly dropping in the Belfast, Antrim and Ballymena areas, and that was not acceptable, especially as the sales had improved monthly in Derry, Coleraine, Omagh, Dungiven and Maghera, which were my areas.

Des also pointed out: 'Joe is not getting the same special offers for his customers, as they are in the bars in Belfast and areas.'

This did not go down well with the other salesman, and definitely not with me. I was neither offered, nor told, about special incentives for the bars, and special price offers. I also found out now that the company were contemplating pulling out of Northern Ireland altogether.

A few months later I was up at the usual monthly meeting, where we delivered our cheques for the pubs sales, and then the boss would hold a meeting about the sales chart. No worries for me there. When I arrived up for the meeting, as I got out of my car, one of the firm's garage mechanics approached me. Joe can you leave your car today for a service, and collect it next week. We will leave you a Peugeot at the front. Fine I said, and handed him the keys. After I came out of the meeting to head home, it was really cold and already dark. The Peugeot 305 car was outside, with the keys inside.

I was glad the meeting was over, as some of the reps were getting a hard time, and the boss always shot from the hip. I was glad it wasn't me getting it, but I did feel for some of the guys' embarrassment.

I headed through the city and on to the motorway home. It was really cold, so I turned the heater on full blast, and waited for the heat to come through. Nothing, just cold air. I turned it off. I was freezing in the car by the time I reached the Glenshane Road, and as I started to climb up Glenshane, it began to snow. I turned on the window wipers, nothing, I was so angry. How could any mechanic let a firm's car out, without testing the heater, and wipers in the middle of winter? The snow was light, so I slowed down and finally made it to the top of the pass. The snow was getting even heavier now, and I knew it would be impossible to drive in. I sat at the top of Glenshane from 6.30pm to 10.45pm before the snow finally stopped. I got out and cleaned the windows with my hankie, all that I had, and made it back home.

The next morning I went out and looked at the car in daylight, it was a heap of junk. I phoned the office, and asked to speak to Des. I told him what happened, and told him I would not be back. He tried to get me to think again, but my mind was made up. I thanked him and hung up. Then I rang reception again.

'Put me through to the garage, please, it's Joe.'
'Hello, garage here.'
'Hello, is that Allen?' I said.
'Yes, who's this?'
'It's Joe, Allen. Just to let you know, I got home safe, but if I see your face again, I will alter it. Goodbye.'

I never went back. I left the car at my door on Monday morning with the keys in it, and they sent a man to recover it.

No, not Allen, I watched them take it.

Sometime after that, within a year, Scottish and Newcastle pulled out of Northern Ireland.

Mason's Bar, 1983

In 1983, I was offered the chance to lease Mason's Bar in Magazine Street. It had been closed for several months due to a fire that had engulfed the kitchen area. Now having been redecorated, it was opening again for business.

Once again I employed my old trusted stalwarts, Newell McBride, Garvin Kerr and Pat Lynch who had a lifetime's experience in the trade and his help and advice was always sound and he was looked up to by all who met him. I wanted to get meals going as soon as possible, as during the day that part of the city could have a slow footfall.

At lunchtime the meals started bringing in the office workers from the city centre. The two girls I got in to cook the meals did a great job, and we had agreed they would buy all the food and keep all profits from the sale of the food.

This worked well for both parties as the customers for lunch started coming back at night. There was music in the upstairs lounge ranging from discos to live bands, three nights a week. I also installed a video jukebox in the bar, which had a selection of different genres of music. It was very popular as one of the first installed in a local bar.

I was only in Mason's a few months when I was asked to provide a bar for one night at the Sports Complex on Buncrana Road. It was a snooker challenge exhibition match between Hurricane Higgins and Doug Mountjoy.

The Complex had no licence to sell alcohol and needed a publican to set up a bar for the night. I was delighted and the tickets were quickly sold out.

By now the bar itself was doing well. We even had a bikers disco, playing rock music every Saturday afternoon upstairs in the lounge from 4.00pm to 6.00pm. The bikers had become regulars in the bar. I found the lads to be great craic and very helpful. This shocked many in the bar as it was not what they had been led to believe by stupid stories from silly people. The night of the challenge match, we were all set up and ready for a busy night. The Complex was packed with a real buzz was in the air.

I had Guinness set up and a few draught beers on a mobile counter. It was just stout, Harp and Smithwick's available. It was a bit of a problem changing kegs, as they had to be screwed on with a metal wrench. I asked one of the biker lads that day to bring down a couple of his wrenches from his collection from working on the bikes.

'No prob, Joe,' he told me, 'leave the kegs to me and I will sort any that need changed when they are empty.'

Higgins and Mountjoy were in great form that night and the banter between them had the crowd in the palms of their hands. Shortly after the match had begun, one of the Complex workers informed me that there was a crowd down at the front door trying to get in.

I called my brother Harry who was keeping an eye on the crowd in case any problems would arise, and we went down to the front door. At the door we found a bunch of young lads trying to get in without tickets. I tried to explain to them that it was sold out and was a ticket-only entry. One of the lads produced a large butcher's knife and threatened me to let them in. Before I had time to even blink, this arm came from behind me with a large wrench in the hand and smashed into the wrist of the knife-carrier's hand. My biker friend with the wrench pushed past Harry and me and started to swing the wrench at the rest of the lads who all turned and ran like they had seen a ghost.

The lad who had the knife was still squealing with pain complaining that his wrist was broken as he ran away.

The biker shouted after him, 'Sue me!'

The rest of the night went great and the staff and my biker friend had a few drinks before we all headed home.

Thank you to Mr Harley Davidson.

Desmond's Factory, 1985: My Own Defence

In 1983, I took a break from the bar world. Desmond's Factory in Newbuildings, advertised for a van driver. I applied, and went for an interview. The manageress was a lady called Una McShane. Una had started work in the factories straight out of school. She had worked her way up and knew any job of stitching in any piece of clothing.

She asked my name, and as soon as I gave it, she asked me, 'Is Margaret your sister, worked in Tillie's? And your mother Maggie was an inspector of the clothes?'

I said, 'Yes, they are.'

'That's good enough for me,' she said.

'Your sister Margaret was the hardest, and best girl worker I have ever seen in a factory, and your mother was a perfectionist, when it came to the final product. The job is yours Joe, can you start tomorrow morning at 5.30am?'

'I can start now, if you want, Miss,' I replied.

'I like it already,' she said.

So my sister and mother got me the job. The factory work was so different from the bar. Travelling from factory to factory with materials. Taking jeans to be stone washed, pyjamas, shirts, tee shirts, shorts, to different factories every day. Desmond's had eight factories at this time, and employed approximately four-and-a-half thousand people. The freedom of getting out in the van, rather than being stuck in a bar all day was great.

When there were no van runs to do, I would do odd jobs around the factory. There was another man who was employed there, and had been there for years, Tommy Finn. Tommy was a wee gentleman, and a hard worker. Tommy was in his sixties then, but the girls all adored him. The other van driver was Jerry Friel. Jerry was a Rosemount man, and loved and trained his greyhounds for a hobby. Jerry was full of craic, and always winding the girls up, and a good guy to work with.

One day, while up in Swatragh at a factory, I visited the shops on my lunch break to get cigarettes. I bought a toy wind-up mouse for my son. When I came back to the factory, I was showing it to Jerry.

The most of the girls were all on their afternoon tea break by the time I got back and emptied the van. Jerry, with that mischievous grin on his face, walked toward the canteen door, as he wound the mouse up. As he passed the doors, which were always left open, he simply bent down and sent the mouse straight up in the tables.

If Jerry thought that there would be a bit of screaming, and that would be it, he was way off the mark. When the mouse was spotted, there was screaming like death screams, then the girls jumped up on the tables, and were firing down cups and plates like a Greek restaurant or wedding. When the mouse stopped, they still had to be convinced it was a toy, not a dead mouse. At that time, there were workmen in fixing the ducting on the ceiling, and they got the blame. No more was said of it. I never recovered the mouse.

A few months later, I was driving along the Victoria Road, taking garments to the factory in Springtown. Just before the turn off to the right for the Everglades Hotel, there was a bus in the right-hand lane, indicating to turn off to the Everglades, and behind the bus, a police car. The police were not directly behind the bus, more to the left lane, but were also indicating to turn right. As I reached the police car, I moved slightly on to the slip road at the side, to give the police car room to turn. As the bus turned right, and I passed the police car, they immediately passed me, and pulled me in. The passenger in the police car was the local D.I. The driver of the car approached me and asked for my licence.

As I handed it to him, I asked, 'Why have you pulled me in?'

'You overtook us back there in the inside lane.'

I laughed at him, 'Officer,' I said, 'how can you overtake a parked car?'

'Listen, I'm not going to argue with you, that is the District Inspector in the car, and he says, you did. Now you can admit guilt, or go to court. Which is it?'

'I'm going to court, and you know I did nothing wrong,' I said.

'Right,' he said, as he handed back my licence, 'the D.I. will see you in court, you will receive a summons within six months.'

'Fine,' I said, and as he walked away, I added, 'drive safely.'

He didn't even look back, no sense of humour.

Each week I waited for the post, but nothing, then one morning as I was getting ready to go to work, a knock at the door. It was exactly 5.00am. I opened the front door and two policemen were standing there.

'Are you Joseph Aloysius Nelis?'

'Yes,' I said.

'This is a summons for you to appear at Derry Petty Sessions, if you do not appear, a warrant will be issued for your arrest.'

I closed the door, and sat and read the summons. It was exactly six months to the day, since they stopped me. When I read the summons, I could not believe the story they had come up with.

My wife said to me, after she read it, 'This is serious Joe, you need to get a solicitor.'

I said I would be gutted to have to pay a solicitor, to defend me against this. I already had told Una, the day I was stopped, so I informed her that now it was going to court.

'Have you got your own solicitor Joe, or do you want me to get one for you?'

'No thanks, Una,' I said. 'I haven't even made my mind up yet, if I'm going to get a solicitor.'

'Joe, you need to. If found guilty you could have your licence endorsed and lose it for a period. Maybe even your job, which I would want no part of Joe, but the directors might.'

'If any judge could believe the story they have written, Una,' I said, 'he would need to have an IQ lower than a monkey, and I know Una I have told you the truth what happened so I'm going to let the judge decide who's the liar, and whatever happens, so be it.'

The day before the court case, I was walking down the factory floor, as Jerry was walking up.

'Here comes Perry Mason,' he ripped. 'You're not really going to represent yourself, are you?'

He smiled that Jerry smile.

'Yes, I am,' I said.

'You don't think you stand a chance against the D.I. without a solicitor Joe? You'll be toasted by them. If you were a betting man, I would bet you, you will lose big time.'

'How much, Jerry? I said.

'I had it out before I even thought.'

'Fifty quid for sure,' he said, and produced the money.

'You're on, Jerry, but I have to call at the bank, but I will leave it up in the office with the wages clerk, to hold with yours.'

As he walked on, came the wee comeback: 'A fool and his money…' and he kept walking.

My first run out after that, I went to the bank.

A bet's a bet.

The day of the court case, I was one of the first into the courtroom, and took a seat at the front where the onlookers' seats start. I was dressed in a three-piece suit, shirt and tie. As everyone filed in, I noticed a lot of policemen at the back of the court. Was this normal, or were they here to watch the District Inspector perform?

After the first half dozen cases were over, which seemed to be people charged with riotous behaviour, or drunk and disorderly, a lot of shouting and finger gestures erupted from young people in the seats. The police were probably there in case it got out of hand.

The morning wore on, and at 12.30pm the judge, Mr McLaughlin, adjourned to after lunch, all back at 2.00pm. I went to a nearby café, and had a cup of tea; I needed it. My nerves were starting to tingle. In the court that morning it seemed like, stand up, guilty, take him away. I knew the judge had the name of being very fair. I just hoped I would get a chance to tell my side. I was the first case up, after lunch. The D.I. had a police solicitor, and I came forward, from my seat at the front. The judge asked me if I was I represented.

I said, 'No, your honour.'

'I can appoint you a solicitor, Mr Nelis, if you haven't got one,' he replied.

'No, your honour, I want to do this myself.'

'Very well, if there is anything you don't understand, or you want to question, Mr Nelis, don't shout out, just put your hand up, understood?'

'Understood, thank you, your honour.'

He turned to the D.I.'s solicitor, 'Continue.'

He read out the summons, but when it came to the part of indicating, he said they never did indicate to turn right, as they were to drive straight on.

He said, 'As they were waiting for the bus to turn right, the D.I. looked in the driver's rear mirror, and saw a light blue transit van, behind, coming towards us. It was travelling at approximately fifty-five to sixty miles per hour. As the van came level to the police car, it drove partly on the hard shoulder. We immediately pulled him on to the hard shoulder, and spoke to him.'

He finished by saying that I was being charged with speeding, careless driving, and overtaking a police vehicle on the inside. 'Thank you, your honour,' he said and sat down.

The judge then turned to me,' Mr Nelis, would you like to make your statement now, and do you understand the charges?'

I stood up, and kept the one piece of information that was in my head. A day after I was stopped, I had a cousin who worked in the Everglades, and yes, I knew for certain they were going to a police meeting that day.

'Yes, your honour, I would. I would like to say first, I did not get a solicitor, out of any disrespect to this court. My solicitor Brendan Kearney is in court right now. The reason, your honour, is, I am going to tell you my story of what happened, and the police will tell theirs. After that, your honour you will decide the truth, and I am happy to abide by your decision. Can I ask some questions your honour, or do the police want to ask me any first?'

He looked at their solicitor, who waved his arm towards me: 'Carry on Mr Nelis.'

'Can a passenger in a car see into a driver's rear-view mirror?' And I looked at their solicitor, and waited for an answer.

'I think what the officer meant was, he looked in the passenger's wing mirror,' he replied.

'Your honour, by law, and if I am wrong please correct me, an affidavit statement is sworn to be the truth to the best of one's knowledge. This affidavit statement was written on the afternoon of that day, it cannot be changed now, or does he remember now the facts, six months later than on the day?'

'It was a simple mix up about the name of the mirrors, your honour,' their solicitor came back.

'Then tell me,' I replied, 'was it also a slight mix up on the indicator lights and the headlights that day?'

The police car did not mix up any lights; their solicitor was beginning to get a bit salty, looking at this upstart van driver.

Then I produced the silver bullet.

'Your honour, I have only two more questions to ask, and then I am done. I want to ask the D.I., or his solicitor to answer one question, and to remember, we have sworn to tell the truth today. I then produced a sheet of paper from a folder I had brought with me, and held it in my hand. Had the police and the D.I. arranged for a meeting, that day at 11.00am in the Everglades Hotel? The same day they were sitting at the junction of the Everglades at 10.50am?

I held the paper in my hand, and made it obvious to the judge and police. The solicitor whispered something to the D.I.

'Yes, your honour, but the D.I. was going to the Strand Rd Station first, before returning for the meeting.'

I just smiled over at them. 'Your honour, my last point is this. The D.I. says I was travelling at roughly fifty-five to sixty miles per hour. Yet in the affidavit they say they followed me immediately the bus cleared their way. Even by some miracle one could tell, through looking in a side wing mirror, the average speed of a vehicle coming from behind, they said, they pulled me into the hard shoulder immediately. If, your honour, I was travelling at sixty miles per hour, which is twenty-nine yards per second, in only twenty seconds I would have been on the slope down to the bridge, where there is no slip road. I was pulled up within fifty to sixty yards after I passed them, because I was doing the allowed speed limit. I still had the piece of paper in my hand, which I knew the solicitor was dreading being shown to the judge.'

Then the judge spoke, 'I know that road well.' And he looked at the police solicitor, 'I always thought that the road that you call the hard shoulder, was a slip road, to help the flow of traffic, if the right lane into the Everglades is blocked up.'

Then their solicitor made the biggest mistake of all, 'Ah no, your honour, you're badly mistaken there.'

I immediately chipped in, 'As I was, your honour.'

'And right you were, Mr Nelis. Case dismissed.'

The courthouse was ringing with cheers from all the onlookers, and probably some waiting for members of their families up next.

'Thank you, your honour, so much, and I think I even bowed as I left.'

As soon as I got out, I found a phone box and phoned my wife. She was bewildered to say the least. Now I could not wait to see Jerry, and get my bet, it was like Jerry paying me for representing myself.

Desmond's Factory, 1992: On Your Bike

The short break I was taking from the bar work was turning out longer than I thought. I was enjoying the factory work, and the money was good. At that time, an old friend of mine from the Park Bar days, Martin Ferguson, came to see me. Martin and my brother Harry were doing doormen in the Rafters Bar, and the owner of the bar decided to have music in the Venue Lounge, so they needed another doorman for Friday and Saturday nights. We had our three boys then, Peter, Brian, and Kevin. We had bought a caravan, down in the Downings, so the extra money came in handy.

At this time, Desmond's were opening a cutting room in their Drumahoe factory. And I was asked if I would move to work there. I agreed, as there was a bonus scheme set for the amount cut every week. The cutting room was again very different from the van job. Most days were worked from 8.00am to 8.00pm, but the money was really good, and the banter was great, between all the lads there. After a few months, and some nights out together, there was a close camaraderie built between us. Two men I became close friends with were Ronnie Kennedy and Kevin ('Logie') Logue, and we still are friends today. Ronnie was the most upbeat guy you could ever meet, and sound as a pound. While Kevin was quieter, and always a good listener, and a footballer with Oxford All-Stars.

The two of them came up with the idea of us doing something for charity over the coming Easter weekend, as we had the weekend off, plus Easter Mon and Tuesday. Everyone had very different thoughts as to how we could all do it together. Paddy McCullagh, from Strabane, came up with the idea: we could all meet up for a pint that night, and settle our plan as to what was the best way.

Gerard Cartin came up with the idea to cycle from Galway to Derry, over two days. From Galway to Sligo the first day, and from Sligo to Derry the second. We all thought he'd gone mad. Some of us were in our forties then, and had not been on a bike in twenty years or more, some of us, never.

'Listen lads,' Gerard went on, 'it's the Easter festival in Galway on that Monday. There will be crowds everywhere. Every town we go through will be packed on the streets. When we reach each town, we stop, collect, and cycle on. We stop overnight in Sligo; get a good night's sleep, then on to Derry. Knock, Bundoran, Ballyshannon, Letterkenny – they will be buzzing. We could do this, lads.'

'Oh yes,' I said, 'you could Gerard, you could probably do it in one day, as you're in a bike club, but us, what do you think lads?'

I could see Gerard had got them won. 'Right, you're on pal.'

We all shook hands, and it was settled, and another round was called. The next morning Kevin, Gerard and Ronnie went to our manager, the late Sean Mullan. Sean Mullan was our boss, and one of the kindest men, you could ever wish to meet. A pillar of the Credit Union in Derry from it first started, and a great and thoughtful boss. They explained to Sean about the charity cycle, and that we needed the work van to get us, and the bikes to Galway. We also needed to bring packs of water bottles, and some lemonade, plus snacks to keep the energy up.

'I don't think Nelis and a few of the old boys will cycle ninety-four miles in a day,' he laughed.

They agreed, and explained that there were ten of us, signed up, and we would take five bikes. Five would do ten miles at a time, then the other five would complete five, until we got there.

'Makes sense, don't want you lads back in here on Wednesday morning, walking like John Wayne,' he quipped. Sean wasn't far wrong.

'No problem lads, leave it with me.' And we knew, he was as good as his word.

Not only did Sean get us the van, he phoned the owner of the company, Denis Desmond, and the directors and told them how this would be a great advert for the company, and the media coverage would be great for any job recruit needed. Not for one second did we think that Sean was doing this for the firm's benefit, it was for us to get as much publicity, and raise as much as we could, for the cycle.

He also phoned all the factory managers, and asked them to let all their workers know about the cycle. Sean even worked out the rota, for who rode what bike in what order. So we decided we would ask him to name three charities that the money would go to. I know Sean was really pleased at that. He took a few days to think about it, and he came up with three charities that we felt happy about. The three charities that Sean named were Multiple Sclerosis, Cystic Fibrosis and Muscular Dystrophy.

A week before the cycle we had not been even on a bike for a practice, but what the hell, even the devil hates a coward. Sean was even on the ball with posters he got some firm to do. He needed the names. Gerard Cartin, Raymond Harley, Ronnie Kennedy, Kevin Logue, Paddy McCullagh, Kevin McLaughlin, James O'Kane, Gary McLaughlin, Mark Duddy, and me.

That last day of work, the Friday before Easter, we were finished at lunchtime. The van was outside, at the loading bay. Sean walked out with us, to the bay. We could not believe it. There was a large poster down each side of the van, advertising our marathon cycle for charity, and the charities we were raising the money for. On top of the van, fixed to the roof, was a large loudspeaker, and a mic inside connected to the speaker, so we could let people along the way know, the bikes were coming behind. When we opened the back of the van, there were bottles and bottles of water, lemonade of every variety, and boxes of snacks, which Sean had got the firm to supply, plus a generous donation from the firm. We could not believe all that Sean had done, and all in his own quiet way.

Saturday morning, five bikes, ten friends, and all our drinks, and a change of clothes, not to forget we all brought our favourite music tapes to play, through the speaker on the way. No CD player in the van, just a tape player. We were on our way. Yee-ha!

As soon as we were out of the city, big Ray Harley said, 'Time to rock the road, lads.'

He pulled out his favourite music tape, and stuck it into the tape player. Ronnie Kennedy was driving at the time. We only heard the opening few bars, before Ronnie banged the eject button, and fired the tape at big Ray. 'Are you off your skull? Right now I don't think we need to hear Chris Rea singing "this is the road to hell".'

That was the start of a fantastic three days; already the van was ringing with laughter. We arrived that night in Galway around eight. We didn't book a B&B for that night, just for Monday night in Sligo, we completely forgot. They were all full in Galway due to the Easter weekend.

We were driving down a street when a young lad of around twenty was passing the van. We called him and asked if he knew any B&B's nearby.

He noticed the sign on the van. 'Are you guys doing the cycle tomorrow?'

'Yes, hopefully, if we can get somewhere to sleep tonight,' I said.

'Pull the van forward a bit, to number 82,' he said.

He turned and walked back to the house. 'Come on in,' he called.

A few of us went in. It was a large house, well decorated. 'You can stay here tonight,' he said, 'there's plenty to eat in the fridge and freezer.'

'Who owns this place,' I asked.

'My mother and father,' he said, 'but I live here. I'm at university here, but my family are from Dublin, and I am going home for a few days' holiday.'

'Thank you very much lad, but we can't do that, you don't even know us,' I said.

'I don't have to, you're doing a good deed, and I don't think if you were burglars, or robbers, you would be in a highly visible van, with adverts all over it.'

We were really shocked by this young man's gesture.

'I have to get to the train station now,' he said. 'Hope all goes well lads, and enjoy your stay.'

'Let us run you to the station, that's the least we can do,' I said.

'That would be great,' he said. 'Just leave the key inside the bread cupboard when you're leaving, I have a spare one.'

We dropped him off and when we came back, we decided not to cook, but to head out, and get dinner somewhere. After we had eaten, the lads decided to go for a pint, and then an early night...ha ha.

I went back to the house, as I didn't drink then, just to make sure all was sorted, as we were leaving the town centre at eight in the morning. Most of the lads were back an hour or so later. Then two arrived back and they didn't look well. They thought the food was off, although I thought it was the drink that was off. They were a kind of green colour, not so noticeable if it had been St Patrick's Day; they went straight to bed. By eleven-thirty, all were back except two, Logue and Kennedy, the two twins. I knew it wouldn't be the drink was the problem; Kennedy loved the chatting. I knew I would have to go and find him.

I found them fifteen minutes later in a hotel bar, chatting to some businessmen. There were only about eight left in the bar, and the manageress was trying to close up.

'Right you two, time to go,' I smiled at them.

They were just nicely.

'Hold on, one of the businessmen said, 'the lads were telling us about your cycle for charity. Ronnie here sang us a wee song, the Streets of New York. If you're from Derry, you must be able to sing as well?'

'Sorry,' I said, 'I can't sing, and we need to go.'

'Listen, if you sing one song before you go, I will give you a hundred punts for your charity, and then one of his friends chipped in, and I will give you fifty more.'

'If you heard me sing, you would donate double that for me not to sing,' I replied.

Ronnie and Kevin nudged me, 'Get in there Nelis, one hundred and fifty punts.'

I started singing a Tony Bennett song, I Left My Heart in San Francisco. Thank God, they all joined in, and I got away with it.

I got the money, and as we were walking out, Ronnie turned to me, and he had a big grin on his face. 'Fair play to you Nelis, Tony Bennett got twenty five dollars, for his first solo performance, Frank Sinatra got thirty-five, and they were class, you got one hundred and fifty punts, and you were shite!'

We laughed the whole way back, with the money. Finally we all bedded down, somewhere, and were all up in the morning, ready for the day. We went to a café early and had cooked breakfasts. To say a few needed them would be true. We parked the van in the city centre, and got the bikes ready, we did some collecting from the people passing, and I did some information through the speaker. I also had a collection tin at my window, which I just held out. A lady came up to the van and handed me a twenty-punt note, and said could I do her a big favour. I said, I would do my best, and after she told me, I thought, that's easy to do.

Just then a handful of people came over to the van, and were giving me donations, so the lady left. Then the lads were all sorted, and they started to get ready to go on the bikes. 'Hold on lads, keep collecting, the money is flowing in, that's what it's all about.'

When we left the young lad's house, we had left a note. In the note we thanked him sincerely for his kindness, and left him a hundred punts to get something for himself. I wanted to get as much in now, as we could.

Suddenly I looked around and there was a man standing at the van driver's window, in his pyjamas. 'What are you doing,' he shouts at me, shouting all over the square with that foghorn thing, he shouts. 'I'm in that hotel across the street, and I have a lady with me, and I can't concentrate on her, with all this blaring going on.'

'We are raising money for a worthwhile charity,' I said.

'Right,' he said, and in his hand was a ten-punt note. 'Take this now for your charity, and fuck off.'

'Thank you,' I said, 'but with your attitude and aggression, I may stay for another hour. Now you fuck off.'

As he marched off I told the lads what happened. The lady who gave me the twenty punts asked if I could stay a little longer, as she was with a man, who turned out not to be very nice. She knew he would eventually come down to us, so she would be ready to leave as soon as he came down. The lady appeared back at the van, minutes after he left. Thanked us, and was gone.

What a start to the morning.

Finally the cycle began, with the van travelling in front. The day went well, and the weather was great, sunny with a fresh breeze. As we passed each mile, and got to the next town, the people's generosity pushed us on. Tuam, Knock, Charlestown, Tobercurry, and finally Sligo. Even though we were leg weary, the thought we had made it this far, was an achievement for us older boys. We found our bed and breakfast and were thankful to get a hot shower, change of clothes, and a proper dinner, which was not part of the deal, but the owner supplied it free.

He informed us that there was a lounge bar just up the street, and they had music booked for that night. That was literally up the boys' street. Ronnie reminded them that we had an early start, and we would be all stiff and sore in the morning, no need for a hangover as well. Always the comic Ronnie.

We all went up to the bar around nine, and it was jammed. We got some seats up beside the two guys playing. It was a large lounge; it held about two hundred. It had a large bar along the back wall, and five staff serving behind it. We were enjoying the chat with the regulars; eager to know how we got on, when they discovered why we were there. The two lads playing were mainly being ignored, with their country music songs. After about an hour, they really looked fed up. Big Ray Harley was talking to them between songs.

A couple of minutes later, Ray taps me in the shoulder. 'The guys asked would we give them a wee break.'

Big Ray was a good singer, and had won a singing competition in McLaughlin's Bar in Derry, just a few months earlier. Young Gary McLaughlin was a great guitar player.

'Go ahead, I said, knock them out.'

'I need you on drums, Joe,' he said.

'Great,' I said, 'if there were drums.'

'There's a set behind the curtain from this afternoon, the boys told me.'

So up we went, and sure enough, I pulled the curtain back, and there were a set of beautiful blue, Premiere drums. When we got sorted, I asked Big Ray what he would be singing.

'Let's give them a real bit of rock and roll,' he said.

'Oh, Jeepers, not Chris Rea again,' I said.

'No, Great Balls of Fire,' he replied.

I looked at Gary, 'No problem Joe, just you count us in.'

Big Ray stood with the mic in his hand, with his back to the crowd. The noise in the place started to die down.

I counted, 'One, two, three, four…'

Big Ray just spun around on the stage and belted out, 'You wreck my nerves, and you rattle my brain…'

Then Gary and I came in.

In less than ten seconds, the crowd were on their feet, it was mad. Big Ray was putting on a show, and as he sang, more and more joined in. When we finished the song, the place was bouncing. We went to come off the stage, but the two guys were enjoying their break.

Then the boss came up, 'If you do another couple of songs, I will make a donation, and I will let you make a collection in the bar, when you finish.'

Too good an opportunity to miss this, we thought.

James, Kevin, Paddy, and Gerard were already on their way back down to the van; they came back to the bar with an armful of collection boxes each. We did another couple of numbers, and then made the collection. The customers were great at the giving, and the owner handed us fifty punts as we were leaving. That night we all went to bed at around eleven thirty, and slept the sleep of the dead.

The next morning we were all up early, and left Sligo at exactly eight o'clock. No problems this morning, Bundoran here we come. It was another beautiful day, but it did not ease the pain in our asses.

When we reached Bundoran, it was just a mass of people everywhere. The main street was like Fifth Avenue. The van arrived before us, and the lads were already out collecting in the street and shops. When we got back on the road, young Kevin McLaughlin was not happy. He told us why. He went into a slot machine place and it was packed. He went up to the reception area, and asked the boss if he could make a collection for charity. The boss said he didn't want the punters bothered, but he would make a donation on behalf of the business. He then handed Kevin a fifty-pence piece.

Kevin went into a shop next door, and asked the shopkeeper, 'Could you spare me fifty pennies please.' The shopkeeper obliged him.

Kevin went straight back into the slot shop. He stood just inside the door, then in a loud voice shouted to the boss man, 'You can keep your 50 pence donation, here it is.' And he slung the pennies all over the floor.

'Beat them up you, you know what, a penny at a time.'

We were really shocked, as Kevin is usually so mild. He just kept repeating for 190 miles, 'Fifty pence. The scrooge!'

So on we went, Ballyshannon, Donegal town, when we got to the top of Biddy's Gap we were exhausted. Then I saw a car parked at the side of the road. The lads all started cheering, and I saw my wife and children. They had been waiting there for us coming, and had brought with them soup, sandwiches, salad rolls and sausages rolls. We had a party at the side of the road, and the sight of them, and the food, gave me, and the lads a real lift.

We headed on towards Ballybofey, then Stranorlar, Lifford, and across to Strabane. Gerard Cartin, the only real bike man in the group was something else. As he saw any of the lads fall behind, Gerard would drop to the back, and give them a few words of encouragement, and get them going again. He did this countless times through the two days. The amount of times Gerard went from leading the group to falling back to last, and back to leading the group, he must have cycled fifty miles more than the rest of us.

When we first had the idea of doing this run, Gerard mentioned it to his bike friends in the City of Derry Cycling Club, and he told us they thought we had bitten off more than we could chew. Which was completely understandable. They promised Gerard they would be waiting at the Guildhall on the night, to congratulate us, if we made it. When we hit Derry, and across the bridge, we went up Carlisle Road, so we could finish by going down Shipquay Street. That way the lads at the Guildhall would see us coming.

As we went around the Diamond, Gerard, in front, turned down Shipquay Street, but we stopped. We wanted the lads to think only Gerard had made it to the finish, but also to let the main man come in as the leader. A minute later we headed down, and apart from the bike lads, our families and friends were there waiting. It was just great to be home and finished.

The next morning at eight o'clock, nine of us walked down the factory, just like John Wayne, but it was worth it. The cycle raised almost ten thousand pounds for the charities, and gave us a great weekend of friendship, which I value to this day.

I remained working in the factory until 1999 and, when Desmond factories were closing down, I took voluntary redundancy and left.

The Trinity Hotel, 2000: An Evil Act

I suppose, most of us anyway have said, or done things in our lives we are not proud off.

I think that it would be fair to say that in the vast amount of cases, it is done in the spur of the moment, and not with any forethought of malice. Usually a sincere apology goes a long way to healing the hurt.

Sad to say, in some cases, there seems to be no apology, or contrition.

I was working in the Trinity Hotel at the time, and called into the bar, to collect my working hours rota, for the following week. As I entered the bar, the table next to the door was being used by a good friend of mine, Shaun, and his elderly dad. Shaun's father suffered from advanced dementia. Shaun had brought his father out for the day, and called in for lunch.

I said my goodbyes, and headed up to the bar, and while I was waiting for a member of staff, to get my rota, I was chatting to another two friends of mine, seated at the bar. While I was waiting, I noticed four or five guys at a table. They were causing a real racket, shouting and cursing, and generally being disruptive. One of the bar staff went to them, and told them to leave. They became more aggressive and started shoving the barman. He told them he was phoning the police, and he went back behind the counter.

The threat of the police coming seemed to work, as they started to leave. I was not aware at this time that, only the day before this, two of them had just gotten out of jail. As they were leaving they were shouting obscene remarks to the staff. As the last of them reached the front door, he turned and swung his fist and caught Shaun's father square on the back of the head. Shaun's father fell face down on the floor. When the scumbag (and that's what he was) reached to go to the door, I was only a few steps behind him. I went out the door and reached for him round the neck, and dragged him, kicking, and swinging his arms, back into the bar.

The staff saw what had happened, and phoned the police, and some of them were locking the door, as the scumbag's mates tried to get back in. When I let go of his neck, I told him he was being handed over to the police for assault. He immediately tried to start throwing punches, but I was waiting for him to start. To tell the truth, I wanted him to start, so I could let him feel some of Shaun's dad's pain. Typical of a bully, two slaps and he was squealing like the pig that he was.

The front of the bar was all glass panels, even the front doors, and his pals were smashing the panels to get in. One of them had made a good size hole in one panel, and was trying to get through it. My two friends from the bar, sat on top of the scumbag on the floor, while I grabbed the guy coming through the panel. One sharp punch to the mouth, and he had enough. Just then the police arrived, and arrested them both for assault and criminal damage. It was the two who had only gotten out of jail, the day before.

They were both found guilty of assault and damages. They got six months each, but had to serve the rest of their previous terms of early release.

They say, evil only progresses, when good men turn a blind eye. Thank God my friends didn't that day.

To Declan and Gerry for their badly needed help that day, I am truly grateful.

A few months later the hotel was taken over by the Travelodge Group. I saw an advert in the paper, for a full time fund raiser for the St John of God's Children's Hospitals in Dublin. It was to raise funds for the hospitals, by raising funds in the Derry and Donegal areas. I got an interview, and ironically, the interview was held in the Travelodge in Derry.

I got my job and handed in my notice to the hotel, and two weeks later, started my new job.

St John of Gods, 2000

The job entailed going door to door, round each housing estate in Derry, asking people to donate five pounds a month, or sixty pounds a year to maintain the eighty hospitals spread over Ireland. These hospitals looked after children, who suffered severe mental illnesses or physical disabilities, which need full time care. At that time, there were none of the hospitals situated in the north, but by raising additional money it was their intention to open two new hospitals in the north. One for the Belfast area, and one for Derry/Donegal. As a small thank you, all donations were included in a monthly draw for five hundred pounds. The hospitals were set up by the Brothers of St John of God, in Stillorgan in Dublin. They also run a well-established Drug and Alcohol Rehabilitation Centre in their Stillorgan Centre.

I worked most days from nine in the morning to seven at night, Mon to Fri. Then at the weekend I would do a few shifts over the weekend for Paul in the Bowery Bar. As most of the new donors I signed up simply donated monthly through a bank account, I had to travel each Monday morning to Dublin, and lodge any donations, with receipts, and bank details of new donors. This was usually followed by a short meeting with other representatives who worked in different counties.

On a few occasions I travelled to a few of the hospitals to see the facilities, and the work that the doctors, nurses, physios, and even voluntary staff carried out. I was really impressed by the care the children received, and when I arrived home that day, I decided I would work the weekends as well. I enjoyed my work, and found it very fulfilling.

In between going door to door, I had also arranged, on a one school per week basis, to speak to the assembled teaching staff at the end of the working day. The target each week, expected of each collector, was thirty-five to forty new donors a week. Between the door-to-door sales, and the schools, many weeks I was well above the expected, and the one of donations, was way above the average, against the normal counties. Typical of Derry. As my good friend Eamon Melaugh said, the good hand never stops giving. That sums up Derry in a sentence.

I was there about six months, and one day my boss phoned to say, they were having their big day, the following week, and I was invited up for the day. One day a year, St John runs a morning Pro-Am golf tournament, an afternoon auction, followed by a gala night in a hotel, which on the night, where the main performer would be a world-class singer. Dickie Rock, of the Miami Showband, himself a world-class act was the main organiser of the entire day organised the whole proceedings. One of his family had been a long-term patient at St John of God hospital and his gratitude had taken a very practical form.

I arrived on the day, and what a day it was. Playing in the golf were all well-known personalities from all over Ireland and England. The afternoon was the auction, and the items were fabulous. Sotheby's in London donated a table and six chairs that auctioned for thirty five thousand pounds alone. The items and the prices they went for were staggering, all donated free by companies. The gala night started with a four-course dinner, followed by a dance, there was a one hour cabaret show. The performer was Johnny Mathis. Unbelievable. I stayed overnight in Dublin, and headed home early the next morning. All went well, but as I was heading on the straight, towards Strabane, there was a man on a motorbike in front of me. As I got closer, I noticed he was weaving back and forward, so I slowed right down. He then started to slow the bike down, but kept going from side to side. I thought the man was unwell, when suddenly he slowed right down, and fell off the bike. I stopped my car right behind him, and dived out to help him. It didn't take a brain surgeon to see he was full drunk. He was not hurt. He had been visiting friends the night before, stayed up drinking all night, and then decided to drive home.

I moved him, his motorbike and my car to side of the road and set him down. I asked him where he lived, and eventually he said he only lived a little up the road. I thought I might walk him home, but I was afraid someone passing might lift the bike. I got him into the car and found his house. I got back in the car, went back, locked the car, and pushed the bike up to his house. I didn't have a clue how to start the bike, never mind drive it.

As I pushed the bike up to the gable of the house, an old lady came through the door. The biker looked to be in his fifties, and the old lady looked about eighty.

'What are you doing with my son's bike?' she said.

I said, 'I was just bringing it up for your son.'

'Why didn't he bring it up himself?' she replied.

'Because he was a little intoxicated,' I said.

With that, she lifted her two hands, and started hitting me in the face and head. 'My son doesn't drink, how dare you! 'Suppose you were going to report him to the police? Get away from my house!'

She didn't have to tell me, I was already halfway down the driveway.

As the months passed, I was really committed to my work, and the winter days were made easier by the thought of the children in the hospitals. As the winter passed, and the summer approached, I started working a few days a week in Donegal, then I would drive back to Derry, and do a few hours at night in the town. The only problem with many of the houses I was invited into in Donegal, was that Donegal people are great storytellers, and they love to tell them, so it was a little difficult to get away if the stories were going on a bit long.

At the beginning of October that year, my boss, Chris rang me. He informed me that he was retiring at the end of the month, and asked me to consider taking over his job in Belfast. I would have to move to Belfast, as it would not be viable to travel up and down each day.

I never liked Belfast, to be honest, and did not want to move up there. I promised him I would have a good think about it, and let him know as soon as I could. The following Monday, which was a few days after the phone call, I went to Dublin, for the usual meeting. I told Chris, I would phone him on Friday, and let him know my decision. After the meeting I headed home.

On Strabane's Melmount Road, I stopped at a set of traffic lights, behind a large van. As I waited for the lights to change, I was suddenly flung forward in my seat, and only for my seat belt, I believe I would have been fired through the windscreen. A car had been coming behind me down the road at speed. When the driver tried to brake, the brakes failed, and he ploughed into the back of my car, and slammed my car into the van stopped in front of me. I thought my neck was broken.

I was lifted out of the car by an ambulance crew when they arrived, and was checked out by them, before being taken to the hospital to be x-rayed for broken bones etc. Luckily there was nothing broken, but I was in severe pain, with my neck and back the worst. Thankfully, none of the other drivers were injured.

When I finally got home, I rang Chris, and told him the story. He told me to just rest, and he would call down and visit me, which he did, a few days later.

Two weeks later, I felt I could go back to work. I phoned Chris and told him I would start back on the following Monday. I put the phone down, and it rang immediately, it was my younger sister Sadie.

'Joe,' she said, 'can you get to the hospital, as soon as possible. Billy took a heart attack, and the ambulance took him ten minutes ago.'

Billy was my oldest brother, and a father to me, since our father had died in 1960, when I was eleven.

I got to the hospital, but it was too late.

I had not just lost a brother, but my hero. Billy had always been there for my mother, and all of our family, after my father died. He was a great footballer, and a real family man. Billy in his younger days had been a Derry City and Coleraine player. After he retired, he was a scout for Nottingham Forest in their Brian Clough era, and sent many Derry lads over to Forest as signings.

I knew how our family would be feeling now, but for Billy's wife Bernie and his family, I just dreaded to see their faces. At the funeral mass, there were players from all over England, Scotland, and Ireland, and the full squad of the Forest team were there. It was one of the largest turnouts seen in the town, for a local man, who never pushed into any limelight in his lifetime. It spoke volumes of the man. The day after the funeral I rang my boss Chris, and explained what had happened, and I gave him my notice as immediate. I just wanted to take a break, and spend some more time with my family.

Bowery Bar, 2001: A Good Deed Returned

At this time I was doing a few nights a week, for a friend of mine at the Bowery. Paul Killen, the manager had injured his back, and had to take a few weeks off. He asked me to fill in and I was happy to help. On a Monday night there was a special cocktail night. All at special discount prices. My partner behind the bar on these nights was Damian Healy.

Damian, better known as Dee, was a joy to work with. The best young barman at that time in the town. In my humble opinion.

All the young people heading downtown to the clubs, would call in first to the bar, for a couple of cocktails, before heading on.

They enjoyed the craic with Dee and me, as we fired up a collection of cocktails. About ten-thirty most of the crowd had left, and there were just a few regulars left in the bar. A couple entered the bar. They were a married couple, and dressed like they had been somewhere special, like the Royal Albert Hall, by the way they were dressed. His wife took a seat at a table, and he came to the bar, and ordered two gin and tonics.

I said, 'Take a seat and I will bring them down to your table.'

He thanked me, and left the money on the counter. I took the drinks and change down and set them on the table.

He thanked me, and as I went to leave the table he asked me, 'You're Joe, aren't you?'

I said yes.

'I remember you well,' he said.

When you have worked in bars for years, and done doorman for years, you don't know what's coming next. I looked at both of them, but nothing clicked.

'I'm sorry,' I said, 'I can't say I remember you.'

'I'll give you a clue, the exit door in the Embassy dance hall any help?' he said.

Then it came to me. Back in the eighties, I was doing the door in the Embassy. One night a young couple had tried to get into the dance, when their friends were already inside. They had no work at the time, and tried to get in without having to pay.

The head doorman had been told about it, and sent me up to bring them down to the front exit. As I was telling them they had to leave, they told me the situation they were in, and I could see they were really embarrassed, and were very polite and apologised. I felt really sorry for them, knowing that all their friends were inside the dance.

Before I came up to remove them, the head doorman had given me my night's money. Fourteen pounds. I took out the ten-pound note, and put the four back in my pocket.

'Take that and come down to the pay desk with me. That will pay for both of you, and get you some drinks as well.'

This was the couple. I sat down beside them for a few minutes, and he filled me in. After that night, they went back to college, and both graduated together in technology.

They moved to Australia a few years later. They now had their own tech company in Australia. They were home for a holiday, and had been out with friends, for a meal at a hotel. When they were leaving he shook hands with me, and said, 'Get you and Dee a drink.'

I thanked them both, and in my hand was a fifty-pound note.

Thanks M and A.

Bennigans Bar

2007

I have worked in a fair number of bars over the years, but Bennigans was my favourite, by a mile. The owners, Kevin and his family, the staff, who, like Kevin, always had your back covered, the customers, to a man or woman, showed the staff and other customers respect and courtesy, beyond what you would normally find. During the City of Culture year in Derry, a brochure was produced, twenty things to do in Derry: Bennigans was listed in the top five places to visit. It was described as a 'shoebox bar, with a great atmosphere, and friendly staff'.

Me, myself, always felt that my feet were comfortable in that shoebox bar. I am also proud to say that, during that famous year in the city, when every business was putting on their best, Bennigans bar won the two most coveted awards a bar can win: the Bar of the Year, and the Charity Bar of the Year. A great acknowledgement to the owner, staff and customers, who have supported the bar, and the charities, with real generosity.

I was glad to have finished my working life there, as I had no wish to stand behind any other bar, in any other establishment.

I have worked with a few hundred staff in my time, but when I met Sadie, on my first day as manager in the bar, I felt I had known her for years. Now, years later I can say, with no hesitation, Sadie was a different class from the rest. The Queen of Bennigans. Always a step ahead of me, when it came to it. Out doing her own shopping, Sadie always had two lists, her own, and what the bar needed. On the big nights, the extra change from the bank, and never forgot the buns for a cuppa. Always enquired about the regulars' families, and had genuine concern if a member of any family was unwell.

Sadie was also the soul of discretion, when it came to anyone's private business.

I remember well an occasion which sums up her loyalty to customers. One day a regular called in for a pint, and it was obvious he was not himself. Sadie put up his pint, and he sat down away from the bar, at a table in the lounge. Sadie confirmed to me, he's not his usual self, and she went down to speak to him. After a few minutes, Sadie returned to behind the bar. I didn't ask her anything about what was wrong, I knew better. Then a man at the bar, who had just started coming into the bar a short time, asked for another pint. Sadie served him. What's the craic with your man down there, he asked Sadie. Sadie leaned over the bar, close to his face,

'Can you keep a secret?' she asked.

'Yes Sadie,' no problem.

Sadie smiled at him and replied, 'So can I.'

2008

On Wednesday nights for a number of years, Eugene provided the entertainment. There have been numerous great music nights in the bar, from all over the world. Eugene was the best all round entertainer of them all. The night started with a game of Play Your Cards Right, and this was mixed with music questions, and jokes. After the game finished, Eugene would entertain the crowd with a range of songs for all ages and genres.

Many of the local singers and musicians would be regulars on that night, and treat it as their night out, as most of them would be working over the weekend.

Eugene would also have been the first to offer his services free, on every charity night in the bar, and has played for years, for free, in many care homes in the city. His one-liners are famous, and he was never backward about putting a heckler in his place. Many of the singers and musicians, who turned up, would be called up for a song or a musical piece. Eugene had a great vibe with all taking part.

On one of these nights, a man and his wife came in for the music. I immediately thought they were in the entertainment business, by their attire. The lady was tall with fair hair, and was wearing a full-length red dress, and red shoes. The man was dressed in a black dress suit, with the sling stripes down the trousers legs, a white dress shirt and bow tie.

After the card game was over, and the singing began, the lady called me over, and asked me, if anyone could get up for a song,

I said, 'Yes, do you sing?'

'Mo, my husband is a singer. He sings every year in the Winter Gardens in Blackpool, the whole summer season.'

'Wow, that would be great,' I said. So I took his name.

The only two people I knew who had sung there were Carol Henderson, local girl of the Henderson Music Shop family, and Josef Locke.

I thought to myself, if he is in the same calibre as Carol and Josef, then he will finish the night with a bang. I let Eugene know the craic and he agreed to call him up last to finish the show. The man was delighted at this.

By the time he was next on, the place was buzzing, and looking forward to this star. Eugene gave him a real build up as he announced his name. He received a warm round of applause to welcome him to Bennigans Bar. He was a real professional as he strutted up on stage, and gave a real introduction. A real pro, I thought. He had a few quiet words with Eugene, and then turned to face the crowd, and lifted the cordless mic off its stand.

The music started and I stood there watching in total shock, as did everyone in the bar. The song he started was an old country song of Hank Snow's: I'm Nobody's Child. A song about a child left in an orphanage. A beautiful sad song, but not for Bennigans at 12.30am, at the end of the night.

To make it worse, he was able to come down off the stage, with the cordless mic, and started moving from table to table singing to the ladies. On top of that, he had not a note in his head, or throat. It was excruciating to listen to, but he just kept on singing the song. As he came to the end of the song, he skipped back up to the stage and, when he finished the song, stood with his hands by his side, I think he was ready to take a bow when the applause came.

There were a few slow claps from a couple of customers, but the rest were still in shock.

He clicked the mic back on the mic stand, and whispered to Eugene, 'That didn't go down well, what's wrong?'

Eugene answered, 'I think you're standing too close to the mic.'

He started to shuffle his feet backwards a few inches. 'How far should I move back?' he asked.

'Have you a car with you?' Eugene replied, and not even a smile on his face.

The star stepped down from the stage and him and his wife left. After he went out the door, Eugene spoke to the crowd: 'Josef Locke has left the building.'

2009: A REAL CHALLENGE

The biggest challenge I have ever taken on in a bar came about after having a chat with Eamon Melaugh. Eamon was well known in Derry for his commitment to civil rights through the sixties and seventies. For the last twenty years or so, he has dedicated most of his energy to Action with Effect, a charity he set up to help homeless orphans and homeless families in India.

Eamon was telling me about the work they were doing, and I told him, I would love to sponsor an orphan child. Eamon was grateful, but asked me if I would consider building a school for homeless orphans. He had purchased a building in Haridwar, as an orphanage, and needed a school to give them a chance of an education. On top of raising money for the school, when it was built, we would maintain the school, by paying for teachers, the children's meals, clothes, and school books, pencils, pens, etc.

I asked Eamon for a ballpark figure. 'What kind of money are we talking here Eamon? To build the school, and maintain the first year's needs?'

'£11,000, and roughly £5,000 a year after that.'

I told Eamon I would need to speak to the owner, and the staff and regulars in the bar. This was something not to be taking on lightly, to say the least.

The following Monday night, I had a meeting with the staff, and some of the charity stalwarts. The three amigos, who were Owen Deehan, John Feeney, and Busty Quinn, plus Eugene McCauley, Big Willie McGeady, Terence Quinn, Kenny (The Big Dote) Stevenson, and Brendan Henderson, of Henderson's Music Shop. All had been the backbone of previous charity nights in the bar.

I also invited Eamon down to speak to them. After Eamon had given them an insight to the children's lives, and the costs of our plan, we waited for the feedback.

Busty was the first to speak. 'Just imagine this folks, we are sitting here having a drink one day, and a young man or woman walks into the bar and asks, "Is this Bennigans Bar that had the school in India? I went to that school when I was a child. Now thanks to all of you, I'm a doctor, working in Altnagelvin Hospital. If just one child had a better life, it would be worth it for what we could do now.'

For a few seconds, nobody spoke, like we were all picturing the scene. Then Owen Deehan spoke. 'Let's do it,' he said.

Big Willie McGeady got up and walked out to his car, and returned with a big plastic water bottle, which he quickly placed on the counter, and with a piece of paper, sellotape and marker, stuck a sign on the bottle. 'Bennigans Babies School Donations', and a large 'Thank You Friends' at the bottom.

William slipped the first £10 donation into the bottle, and we were started. Just as the meeting finished, a group of firemen came in the door. They had heard on the grapevine what we had hoped to do. They had a whip round at the Northland Road station and the Waterside station, and handed over £200. What a start, the excitement was tangible. We were not deluding ourselves, the real work was ahead of us, but it's Bennigans.

The next day, I posted a notice in the bar, and asked anyone who wanted to help in any way, would they please come to a meeting in the bar, the following week. The night of the meeting the bar was packed to the rafters, or would have been, if there had been rafters in the bar. There were people there who I had never met in my life, but just wanted to help. We formed an entertainment committee, and a daughter of a regular, who was the postmistress in Frank Long's post office, would oversee all donations and money events. Brendan Henderson and John Feeney were solely responsible for banking and withdrawals. It was decided we would begin with a charity night in the bar, followed by a dinner dance in the Guildhall.

We hoped to raise between £1,000 and £1,500 to get us a good start. What a night it turned out, and it just got better as the night went on. On the night we had a back-to-back (talent competition), customers versus staff. The customers went all out to win. Busty Quinn, as Garth Brooks, John Feeney as Dean Martin, and Terence Quinn as The Big Dote; then Ann Healy, who stole the show as Susan Boyle. All dressed in the star-styled clothes. Sadie, Mickey McGuinness and I, didn't stand a chance.

We also ran a auction, and the donations included phones, children's rideable cars, a new racing bike still in the box (from Eugene), watches, jewellery, shopping vouchers, paintings, spirits, wine, meal vouchers – it was truly amazing. The gentleman who won the bike raffle donated the bike back into the auction. Mr Grace by name, and by action. The atmosphere was hard to describe by this point, and then to finish the night, Terence Quinn and his son came out of nowhere dressed as Stavros Flatley and Son, and just absolutely took the atmosphere to a new level, with their version of their Greek dancing. A truly unforgettable night. On that one night, in a shoebox bar, and the generosity of everyone, we raised a total of £6.040-00. We were all flabbergasted. Completely!

The next day we counted the bottle, over £800-00.

As the weeks passed, the regulars kept raising money by different methods. Kevin McCafferty, one of the dart players, and an Eric Bristow fan, had been to one of Bristow's exhibition nights, and won a dartboard signed by Bristow. The next day Kevin arrived in the bar, and donated it to the charity.

Kevin O'Donnell, a young man, disabled physically, and wheelchair bound, decided to fly a glider plane in Eglinton, followed by him completing a wheelchair push round the Craigavon Bridge, and back over the Foyle Bridge. Kevin raised £1,500 with his own efforts. His nickname for me was Mr Know-All. On my birthday, he bought me a tee shirt, with the motto: 'If you want to know, Google Joe.'

I went out the back of the bar, took off my shirt and tie, and put it on. I marched back in, and said, 'Thank you Kevin, I really like it, you're very thoughtful.'

'Do you really like it?' he said.

'Yes, I do,' I replied, as I moved to serve a customer.

Suddenly there was a burst of laughter. As I moved away, Kevin turned to his company and said, 'He's still an ugly so-and-so.'

I still miss his company and wit.

Now for the dinner dance in the Guildhall in September. We all knew it would be hard to top the night in the bar, but we were all determined to give it our best shot. The tickets for the dance were £20 each, including dinner. From the minute they went on sale, they went like wildfire. We also had a hundred posters printed, which, like the three hundred dance tickets, were donated by Kevin Clifford, of CityPrint, as he did on numerous occasions for our charity nights.

It was decided by the committee that we would have a large raffle on the night. Again, the prizes donated came as a shock to everyone. The prizes ranged from a two-week holiday anywhere in Ireland, a large television, music systems, etc. Thirty-two prizes in all, given by donation. It was truly overwhelming. Again, the musicians in the town did themselves, their families and the city, proud. From the late, great Eamon Friel, to the Foyle Showband. A number of businesses in the town sponsored a table, for £50. So we put an advert for them on their table. A number of taxi firms supplied £5 free taxis, for a free run home.

Then, once again, Busty Quinn came and told me that he was going to supply all the food, and him and his wife would cook it. This would be his family's donation. What a fantastic job they did.

Harry, my brother, rang me to say he had ten handpicked doormen for the night. Their fee was Busty's dinners, and a drink at the end of the night. A week to go and it was all coming together. A day later I had a visit from Laura Doherty. Laura is well known in the town, as a great singer, and dancer. She thought it would be a real bit of fun to do a scene from the film Sister Act, with men instead of women. We thought the craic would be great, so we all agreed. One man, Lexie McGarrigle, from the Fountain Estate, was all up for it. Lexie was a real legend in Bennigans, and even though he was in his later years, was talked into taking a role. We got seven volunteers and I was the last roped in. Probably because I have two left feet.

I agreed, I would do it, but only if Laura and Lexie took the two main roles. They agreed, and it was agreed we would practice each afternoon, till the day of the dance.

Every day on Radio Foyle, we had great support from our local radio station, Radio Foyle. I would like to say a sincere thank you to Colm Arbuckle, big Mark Patterson, Sean Coyle, Stephen McCauley, and all the receptionists, especially the one and only Janet, for the support and encouragement, over many years, for our charity nights. Special mention to Mark for compering our night in the Guildhall, with such genuine warmth, and good humour, and again the following year's dance, in the Memorial Hall, when Colm and Mark both took part in the band. Not forgetting Stephen, and our Rock and Roll night of music in Bennigans. Thank you all.

The nuns' act, two days before the dance, was still a mess, but Laura would not give up. God bless her.

The night of the dance came, and I could not have wished for better. The crowd were really up for it. The atmosphere, music, food, and the prizes, all first class. That night there were two people who stole the show, Lexie had the hall in stitches with his remarks, large plastic bottle of stout in one hand, a large cigarette holder, with fag in it, in the other. His dancing and loud remarks were even better as his habit was the only one, in mini skirt fashion.

The second star was a Derry man who had been away in London for years, singing on stages with stars. He was an eighty-five year old tenor, Neil Carlin, who had specially flown in, to perform for us, seventy-five years after he had last sung in the Guildhall as a boy. His second last song was Nessun Dorma, followed by My Way. He was just an unbelievable singer, and got a standing ovation that lasted for over four minutes.

Just a night to remember. I always will, and I am, and always will be grateful to anyone and everyone, who helped, even in the smallest way. Thank you to them all.

When the money was counted we were way ahead of our target, and well into our second year target.

The following summer I travelled to India, with four volunteers from Action with Effect. When we arrived in Haridwar, where the school was built, I could not believe the poverty I witnessed.

Haridwar is one of the poorest cities in India. There were hundreds of children begging in the street. It was soul destroying and awful to watch.

When we arrived at Bennigans School, the next day, it was such a vast difference to see these children: clean clothes, healthy, full of energy, each one with their books and bags. At around midday, the children all received a hot lunch, and clean bottles of water. A doctor, called Dr Bashera, gave the children regular check-ups, and the teachers just loved the children.

Later that day, we walked into the city centre. It was a hell on earth. The traffic was bumper to bumper: lorries, cars, motor bikes, scooters, bicycles weaving out and in; cows and goats loose, with no one seeming to own them. In the middle of all this mayhem, children as young as five, were begging food or money off the drivers. The noise of the horns of the lorries and cars would have made you wish you were deaf.

After a few days spent with the children, and a day trip to a waterfall and park, we took them all to a McDonald's, and they each had a Happy Meal. It was better than any Christmas Day.

After we checked out the orphanage, we decided to visit six leper colonies, and brought enough food to help them over the next few months. The colonies were all pieces of barren land, with nothing, no shops, no people, nothing in sight. They lived in tents, made of black bags. They were called Untouchables. The leprosy had taken a terrible toll on their bodies. The loss of fingers and thumbs, to arms, legs, was heart breaking. There were many just laying on wooden boards, just waiting to die. No help from hospitals or government. They were completely ostracized by everyone. We sat and ate with them, and as we were leaving each one, who was fit, gave us a hug and thanked us.

The only way to get leprosy is by drinking contaminated water. How can any government justify wanting to send rockets to the moon, at a cost of billions, not supply clean water for their own citizens? Thanks to the dedicated work by Eamon, and his Action with Effect volunteers, plus the generosity of many people in Derry, some of these colonies are improving.

Eamon has a large number of the colonies fitted with small brick buildings, each about the size of a garage. Each one was fitted with clean water, small stove, and beds. Above the door of each one, was a small plaque, with the name of the family who sponsored it. This on top of ten schools and an orphanage. I have no doubt, the action of Eamon, and the kindness of the people of Derry, has saved hundreds, and maybe thousands, of children's lives in India.

I spent one day in Agra, before I travelled to Delhi, to fly home. Agra is famous for the Taj Mahal. I sat on the same seat that Princess Diana made famous in photos.

As I sat and looked at this beautiful structure, all I could see was the faces of the street children, and the lepers.

2010: STORY TIME

Sunday nights in the bar were quiet after about 10.00pm as the usual Sunday night customers had an early night to prepare for work on Monday. At this time, we did not have Sunday night entertainment. Only a few bandsmen who had the night off, and a few regulars, would sit on for the last hour. They would each tell a story or joke. The craic was great and the atmosphere was like a family gathering.

One of my favourite storytellers was a local singer called Paddy McCafferty. Paddy and Carlinn Bradley were well known in the city as the band, Venice. Paddy excelled at songs from Roy Orbison to Joe Dolan and Carlinn was great at Country to Pop. One of Paddy's stories that stuck in my mind, I will relate here.

Paddy's Story:

Hughie owned a small farm in Donegal. It was handed down from his great-great grandfather. Hughie never married and he was the last remaining member of his family.

Hughie's only friend was Mary who had a small farm also, a few miles from Hughie. Mary also had never married and was the only member of her family left. A few nights a week, Hughie would drive his Morris Minor over to Mary's farm and they would share a pot of tea and a wee chat. They both enjoyed the company and to share how each of their days had been.

One night after work as Hughie was having his tea, before calling with Mary, he heard a piece of news on his radio that shocked him. The government had brought in a new law. If anyone died and had no immediate family, the government would take their farm, house and any property belonging to the deceased and sell it, and the proceeds would go to the government. Hughie was devastated. How could they do this, as his farm had been in the family for generations? Hughie was not letting the government get his farm. He must speak to Mary and ask what she thought of his plan, and he had a plan.

After he arrived at Mary's and they were having their cup of tea, Hughie told Mary about the new law. Mary was absolutely livid and asked Hughie what they could do.

'Well, Mary,' Hughie began, 'we have always been close friends and I have always admired you. If we were to get married and anything were to happen to me, you would get my farm, and I would be so happy knowing that. If, God forbid, anything should happen to you, I would get your farm.'

Mary thought about his plan for a few minutes and then with a smile agreed to it. Mary was twelve years younger than Hughie, which may have helped her to agree to the plan. Over the next few weeks, they made their wedding plans.

As the wedding day drew closer, Hughie began to worry about his feet problem. From Hughie was young he had always a foot odour problem and nothing seemed to take the bad smell away.

Unknown to Hughie, Mary also had a problem with her breath. Hughie knew nothing about Mary's problem, as he had never been close enough to her to notice. Mary knew the honeymoon would end that. Separately, they each decided on how to overcome their secret worries.

The day of the wedding arrived and it was a great success and their neighbours and old friends were all there. They were booked into the hotel where their reception was held and when bedtime arrived, Hughie was the first into the bathroom.

He immediately took off his shoes and socks. He washed the socks in the sink with hot water and soap, repeatedly. He then gave his feet a good wash in the bath for ten minutes, then dried them and sprayed them with aftershave lotion. He then hung the socks on the outside of the windowsill to dry for the morning. He then undressed and had a quick wash before putting on is new pyjamas. He then splashed himself all over with aftershave and walked back in to bedroom feeling like Clark Gable.

Mary did not even take time to look at him. She dived straight past him to the bathroom. Mary immediately took off her clothes and had a wash. She then put on her new nightie. For the next twenty minutes she brushed her teeth and used all kinds of mouthwashes. Finally Mary came out of the bathroom and got into bed beside Hughie.

Hughie looked at her and smiled. 'You look lovely Mary,' he said.

Mary leaned over and gave him a quick kiss.

'Hughie,' she said, 'I have a little secret I have to tell you.'

Hughie stopped her. 'Mary, I have a secret too, and I want to tell you mine first.'

'No,' said Mary. 'I want to tell you mine first.'

'Mary,' said Hughie, 'I know your secret – you ate my socks!'

Just one of Paddy's gems.

2011: NEVER JUDGE A BOOK

Friday evening in Bennigans, one of the best times for real banter.

A good number of the regulars just finished another week's work. It was a good mixture of age groups, and workers and business people. I think that was a great mix for great craic. The golden rules of no politics and no religion discussion, and never ask to watch a Celtic v Rangers match. The regulars respected them, to the man and woman.

It was just an evening like this. When the front door banged open, and a young man walked in. He looked to be in his early twenties. He looked at the customers and then the lounge. 'This is a pukey wee bar,' he sneered. Everyone turned to look at him, and you would have heard a pin drop in the bar.

He then turned his gaze on me.

'Hi you, give me a pint of Carlsberg,' he asked, a bit loudly.

'Excuse me, are you speaking to me,' I asked.

'Aye, who do you think I'm talking to?' he replied.

'Sorry, friend, you're not getting a drink here, so you need to leave right now,' I said, loud enough to let everyone in the bar hear it.

'You're refusing to serve me, why's that?' he smirked again.

'Simple,' I said, 'look around you, friend. These are all nice people, and I don't want, or need, someone with your attitude. So please leave now, and don't come in here again.'

He moved closer to the bar and leaned towards me. 'Are you telling me, I'm barred?' he asked.

'Yes,' I said.

'How long am I barred for?' he asked.

I leaned over close to his face. 'Ninety-nine years,' I said.

'That's grand, you won't be here when I come back,' he said and smiled.

As he turned to walk out, I called to him, 'Did you say Carlsberg, friend?'

The regulars looked at me as if I had lost the plot. The young man was the most shocked of all. He took his pint and sat down on his own in the lounge. When Newell came in to start, I went down with a drink, and had a chat with the young man, and this was what he told me.

He was from the country. He only drank at a small local pub in his area. He would tell the old men in the bar, that he wanted to go into Derry some night, and have a drink in some pubs here. The old men told him, if he came to the pubs in Derry, as soon as they knew he was from the country, the Derry boys would walk over him, and he probably would get a beating outside one of the bars. So, when he decided to give it a try, he came with the attitude, nobody was going to walk all over him, but just took it too far.

Since then, he has been in many times, and a kinder lad would be hard to meet.

2011: SHIRTS AND TIES AND DIFFERENT VIBES

Looking back now, I realise that my first thoughts of working in the bar business, came from watching my brother Jim. Jim worked in the old City Hotel, as a waiter, in the fifties. He was always dressed to perfection, white shirt, bow tie, cufflinks, silver or gold shirt bands, and black trousers. When going to work, he wore a black camelhair coat, and kid gloves. He looked like one of those film star detective movies, from America.

I loved sitting at night in the house, after he finished his shift, and he would tell me stories about some of the famous people who had stayed there. People like Leon Uris, the writer, who had written famous books like Exodus, and Trinity. Paul Robeson, the world famous singer, who was performing all over the world, at that time. He performed the classic song, Old Man River, to a standing ovation in the Guildhall. Joe Loss and his Orchestra, probably the greatest dance band in the world, at that time also.

From a very young age, I was into music, big time, and when Radio Luxemburg started playing the top twenty selling records of the week, every Sunday night from 11.00pm to midnight, I was allowed to stay up and listen. My highlight of the week, for a nine-year-old.

Changed times indeed. Between Jim's stories and, a few years later, when my older brother Johnny was working as a doorman in the Corinthian Ballroom, and hearing of the stars who appeared there, I was never bored as a kid; always great stories in our house at night. So even back then, I think I knew I would be drawn to the hospitality trade.

I know now, it's the normal to wear tee-shirts of all colours behind the bar for staff, but I never got away from wearing a shirt and tie. I never wanted to and on several occasions while working as a part timer, reps would come into the bar on business, and start explaining their visit, I would say to them, 'Oh, it's the manager you need to speak to.'

'Oh, I thought you were the manager, you look like one.'

'Just the shirt and tie, friend,' I would reply.

One other thing that I believe I possess, is an inner vibe, when something or someone is going to cause a bad situation. This vibe is hard to explain, but it's there, and over the years it has stood to me, in many situations. Funny thing is, my youngest son, Kevin, who spent a few years, working with me in Bennigans, has it as well. This was brought home quite clearly, on one occasion, in the bar.

It was around eight o'clock at night, and I came in to begin work. Sadie and Kevin had already started. It was a Wednesday night, Eugene was playing later that night in the lounge, so we expected the crowd later. As I walked in and took off my coat, I started to get this vibe. There were only about six or eight customers in the bar, at this time.

My son Kevin came over and asked me, 'Are you okay, you look worried?'

I said, 'I just have a bad feeling, Kevin, but don't know where it's coming from.'

'It's coming from the man reading the newspaper, at the bar – I felt it as soon as he came in,' said Kevin.

I looked at the man and he was just reading, and drinking his pint, and taking nobody on. I walked behind the bar, and down to the lounge, and as I walked past him, I knew Kevin was right. I could feel it now, even stronger. I just carried on as normal, and hoped I was wrong.

Sometime later, a group of ladies came in; they were regular Wednesday night fans of Eugene. They took a table in the lounge, and Kevin took their drinks to their table. I went out to the smoke area, to check for any empty glasses, and to empty ash trays, and clean any tables needed wiped, all clean, Sadie was way ahead as usual. So I had a cigarette, before the crowd were due in.

As I was going into the bar again one of the ladies approached me at the back door.

'Joe, can you ask the man at our table to leave us alone please?'

'What man?' I asked.

'The one who has come down from the bar,' she said. 'He is really offensive, and his talk is gross.'

'Leave it with me, I will sort it immediately,' I said.

I sent her in the back way, and I went in through the bar. I went straight to their table, and told the man, who was the one reading the paper, that I wanted a word in private with him, up at the bar. I spoke low into his ear, not to embarrass him.

He got really aggressive and, in a loud voice said, 'Anything you have to say, say it here, now.'

'It's private sir, I just need a word with you,' I said.

'I'm not going anywhere, till I drink my pint.' And he was getting more and more angry.

I lifted his pint, and walked up and sat it on the counter. He was following, right behind me. I turned and faced him, 'You have to leave now, sir,' I said.

Kevin was standing behind the bar, ready in case his old dad was in trouble, and Sadie handed the man his money back for the pint, as she lifted the glass, in case he would use it as a weapon.

'Now sir, there is your money back, just leave and that way, you will not be embarrassed further,' I said.

He was now bubbling with anger, and started to lift his fist.

'If you lift your hands to me, sir, I assure you, they will be digging you out of the wall behind you, as I will paste you all over it, I swear,' I said.

He made for the front door, and as he went out, he pulled it so angrily behind him, it was a miracle it was still on its hinges.

After he left, and Kevin, Sadie and I were chatting, Sadie said to Kevin, 'Your father is never wrong when it comes to this kind of vibe.'

We were all relieved it did not come to something worse.

2012: A RANDOM ACT OF KINDNESS

Sometimes, as in all walks of life, you get a chance in the bar game, to do an act of kindness. Sometimes it's a simple thing like giving someone a lift home, when there is a family emergency, or a bit more complicated, like taking a young woman to hospital who went into early labour in the bar. Which I am glad to say, only occurred once.

It is a nice feeling to know you helped someone, no matter how little it takes.

One particular Friday night in Bennigans, there was the usual crowd, plus the three amigos, John Feeney, Busty Quinn and Owen Deehan. They were always good for a bit of banter, and no better men for supporting the charities in the bar, over the past number of years.

Around eight o'clock, a man in his early fifties came in. He was a stranger to the bar. 'Hello, what can I get you?' I asked.

'A double whiskey and soda, please,' he replied.

I explained to him that I never sell doubles.

'Please,' he said, 'I need it.'

I put the drink up, and he paid me. As I was handing him his change, I could see that he was not in a good way.

'I hope you don't think me forward sir, but you don't look well, are you okay?' I asked.

He did not touch his drink, but started to tell me his dilemma. He was a self-employed haulier. Over the last six months he had been unable to work, due to an operation, and ill health. His mortgage, and lorry payments were behind and he stood to lose both. Tonight he had his best job in years. His lorry had broken down, up the street from Bennigans. He thought it was engine trouble. His lorry was full of freight, wood, beer kegs and all other kinds of materials for deliveries to Dundalk, Dublin and Waterford. By now he was in tears.

'If I had delivered that stuff by tonight and tomorrow, I would have had enough money to square everything, and a nice bit left, for my family.'

With that he poured the soda into the whiskey, and was about to take a gulp.

'Please don't touch that drink,' I said. 'Just give me a couple of minutes, to speak to the lads. Maybe we can help.'

I went and told the lads the story, and I am deadly serious, when I say the next hour, was like something out of a movie, and a classic one at that. Firstly, we knew plenty of mechanics, but on a Friday night was not a good night to be wanting one quick. Secondly, what if the engine could not be sorted, then we would only be wasting time.

Busty and Owen both looked at John. 'Don't touch any more of your beer, John,' Owen said, and then they set to work.

John phoned a taxi to take him to his sister's recycling plant business, where they kept their lorry, which John drove. Owen got on his phone and phoned his forklift driver, at their shipping depot in Eglinton, and told him to bring it to Bennigans ASAP. Busty, John, and Owen then phoned their families, to let them know. Busty and John had first-class heavy goods licences, so they told the wee man they would go with him, and share the driving.

I explained to the wee man that we had a lorry coming, and a fork lift truck and driver. John's lorry would not be needed till Monday. So, they were going to transfer the load from his lorry to John's, and he could make the journey tonight. He was crying and laughing at the same time.

The lorry arrived, and then the forklift. I phoned up to the chippy up the street, and got four large burgers and chips delivered to the bar. When they had all the freight onto John's lorry, and securely strapped down, they ate the burgers with mugs of tea. Owen as well, even though he was not travelling with them, but I knew Owen loved his burgers, and I knew the boys needed the feed for the journey.

When they were ready to go, I called the wee man to one side, and gave him sixty pounds in case he needed diesel on the journey. He did not want to take it, but I told him he could pay me back, if they got the job done. As they pulled away, the customers were all out to wish them a safe journey. Busty said he would keep us updated. Through the night as well, I shouted to Busty. It was a clear beautiful night, as they drove off, and I prayed to God to keep them safe.

I went back into the bar and finished the shift. Got home to my flat around one-thirty. Still no word from them. Around two-thirty my phone rang, it was John. They had Dundalk sorted after dropping off a load, and picking up another load for Dublin and Waterford.

'Ring you later, all good so far,' he finished.

A sigh of relief from me, but could not even think of going to bed. Put on the late all night news, and poured myself a Bacardi and Coke. Nothing on the news interesting; changed channel to late night music, more relaxing.

The hours passed slowly, and all I could hope for was the roads would be a lot quieter at night. Early that morning, Busty rang, Dublin sorted, and another load on for Waterford.

'Had to knock garage owners up, to get diesel. All good so far, Joe. Keep her lit, see you tonight, all being well Joe. John driving.'

Could they pull this off? God help them please, I said to myself. That afternoon, John rang; the wee man driving, 'Hi Joe. On our way home, all went well so far. Hope to be in Derry around nine o'clock. Get the beers chilled, bye.'

That night the bar was waiting for the return of the amigos. Owen had got a mechanic up first thing that morning and had the wee man's lorry sorted after a few hours work. At just after nine that night the lorry arrived, to the cheer of the crowd, and the relief of everyone.

Busty and John got out, and the wee man called to give them whatever they wanted. 'I will be back in an hour with the lorry, Joe.'

I put the two lads up a drink just as Owen came in and joined them. The buzz was overwhelming. Sure enough just over an hour later he arrived, smiling from ear to ear. 'Give the lads what they want, and the staff, and give me a whiskey and soda.'

He was sitting now with the three amigos and he looked like he was in heaven. He told me he had brought John's lorry back with him, and he would get his lifted to a garage, first thing on Monday morning.

I let Owen give him the good news about his lorry being fixed. He was nearly crying again. 'Give the whole bar a drink, Joe, I mean it, put the drinks up for everyone.'

'No chance,' I said, 'you can buy the boys a drink or a couple, but that's it. No more debate about it.'

He insisted I would sit with them and enjoy a drink. There was plenty of staff to cover the shift, so I did. As we were all sitting together, he looked at us and said, 'Tell me boys, what other street, could you break down on a Friday night, and witness an act of kindness like this.'

That night, I felt privileged to sit in the three amigos company. Men, who did not accept a seeming lost cause, but decided they could do something to help a man and his family. This is only one act of kindness, in a list of many that the three amigos were part of.

Something their families should remember, and be very proud of.

2012: BLIND MAN'S BLUFF

It would be very easy now, looking back, to remembering all the bad times and bad days one has to deal with. The bombs, bomb scares, robberies, not to mention the arguments, rows, and sometimes fights, seem to fade to the back of the memory, and I always remember the good times first.

These were all part and parcel of working through the decades of the troubles. I just loved going to work every day. I know some of my friends who were in the trade hated it, it was just a job, they would always say. Not for me, and it never was. The meeting people, banter, debates, big nights, I loved it all.

If in a debate your argument was proven wrong, I always followed my defeat by saying, 'I love being wrong, because of the pleasure it brings to the customers.'

I will give you an example of this.

Every Thursday afternoon, Angus would call in for a pint or two. Then when he was ready his daughter would come and lift him and take him home.

Angus had finished his second pint, and had rung his daughter to collect him. He left to wait outside for her. As he was waiting, a friend of his, who he hadn't seen for a couple of years, was walking down the street with his dog. They chatted for a couple of minutes, and Angus asked him to come back into the bar for a drink. The friend agreed, so Angus phoned his daughter back, and told her to call in an hour.

Then Angus remembered there were no dogs allowed in the bar, only guide dogs.

'Have you been in here before?' Angus asked him.

'No,' his friend replied.

'Right,' said Angus, 'pretend you're blind.'

I was surprised to see Angus back again, as I thought he would be halfway home by now.

'Joe, this is my good friend Roland, who I haven't seen for a couple of years.'

'Glad to meet you, Roland.'

'Two pints of Harp, Joe,' please, said Angus.

'Will do Angus,' I replied.

I poured the drinks, and let them get on with catching up.

I was doing some cleaning behind the bar, when Angus called, 'Two more pints, Joe.'

It was only then as I sat the drinks on the counter, I saw the dog.

I nodded to Angus, and then nodded to the dog.

Angus leaned over to me, and quietly told me, 'He's blind Joe.'

I started to chat to them, and then I said to Roland, 'I do some voluntary work for the Blind Society, did you lose your sight, or were you born blind, Roland?'

'I lost my sight about five years ago,' he said.

'How long have you got your guide dog?' I asked.

'Two years next month,' he replied.

'I'm only asking because normally guide dogs are Labradors,' I replied.

He looked straight ahead but leaned down with one hand towards the cocker spaniel and said, 'Why, what did they give me?'

The three of us just laughed, and we chatted some more.

Angus and I had many a laugh just recalling that day.

2012: HALLOWEEN NIGHTMARE – TAKING RESPONSIBILITY

When I started working in bars, I learnt very quickly, to take some of the responsibility for what you are serving. Alcohol is a legal drug, which can be sold in bars, restaurants and off licences, but it is still a potent drug. In the vast majority of cases, taken in moderation, it can help people to relax, and ease their stress level. It can help shy people to mix, and chat easier in company. It can even make some men and women believe they are Fred Astaire and Ginger Rogers on the dance floor. There are other people who drink does not agree with. It may be due to a chemical imbalance in their body, or their mental state. Therefore I have always felt a responsibility to every customer I have ever served, to be vigilant, and caring for their wellbeing.

Back in the seventies, off licences started becoming more and more popular. Young adults were buying the drink, and their younger friends, who were too young to get served in the bars, had access to alcohol, and were able to go to flats of friends, or parks, and consume the alcohol. This, I believe, led to the young drink culture in the city.

There were no adults or barmen to monitor their consumption, or behaviour; the big brother effect was gone. Sometime around 1974/75, I met a good friend of mine, the late Billy Caldwell. We were chatting and the subject came up about the amount of problem drinkers in the city.

He told me about an idea that he and his wife, Kathleen, and Denis Bradley, along with some other people had been organising. They were going to open an alcohol and drug abuse centre in Derry. They had acquired a building on the Northland Road, and the centre would be named the Northland Centre. I said to Billy how glad that news was, as it was badly needed. Through working in the bars, I had seen some of the problems that drink caused, but had no knowledge of the drug scene.

I said to Billy, 'Is the drug scene bad in Derry, Billy?'

I will never forget his answer. 'It's not that bad yet, Joe, but if it keeps going, in a few years' time, trying to solve the drug problem in Derry will be like trying to empty the Foyle River, with a teaspoon.'

I worked with Billy on several projects to help to raise money for the centre, and he, his wife Kathleen, Denis and all the staff over the years, can be proud of the hundreds of people they helped to a better, healthier life, with their families.

Only once, in my whole working life have I seen the horror of a drug incident.

It was Halloween night, and like every bar in the town, we were packed, and I closed all the doors before we were overcrowded. Around ten-thirty, there was a loud banging at the front door. I didn't hear it with the music and singing, but a customer drew my attention to the door.

I went to the door and called out, 'Sorry, we're full up, no more entry.'

The voice came back, 'Help me please, I need help, I'm bleeding badly.'

I took the lock and bolt off the door, and opened it. There was a young lad standing there, with a ripped white top, and a pair of blue jeans. He was covered in blood, as were his clothes, and he was bleeding from the throat and arms.

I stood staring at him, thinking this was a Halloween wind up, when suddenly he just collapsed, and I was just able to catch him before he hit the tiled floor. He was freezing cold, and I shouted at the bar staff to help me, and for Newell to ring for an ambulance. I grabbed towels and glass cloths from behind the bar, and made tourniquets for his wrists and used the towels to try and stem the flow of blood from his throat. He started to lose consciousness, and I swear I thought he was going to die, by the amount of blood he had lost. I looked up and the crowd were all watching him. I told the staff to clear the bar, so the paramedics would have some room. The truth is, I did not want people watching this young man die.

By now he was a pale colour, but I could still feel his heart beat. Suddenly, I could hear the ambulance siren coming down the street. They came straight in and took over. Minutes later they were on their way to the hospital with him. The staff and customers outside were like nervous wrecks – as was I.

The next morning I rang the hospital, and asked if there were any news. They just confirmed he was fine, but gave no more details.

Two weeks later, I was getting the bar ready to open, when there was a knock at the door. It was the young lad from that night. It was like seeing a lost son. He came in and we had a cuppa, and he told me what happened that night. He had been invited up to a party in a flat on Bridge Street. He had a few beers, but there was a guy there taking drugs. The guy taking the drugs started hitting his own girlfriend. The young lad got up to try to stop him, and a couple of guys turned on him. The drug guy went at the lad with a knife, and as the young guy tried to stop him, he got his arms slashed a number of times. Then they threw him out onto the street.

'Thank God, Joe, I am fine now, but I just wanted to call in to thank you.'

I wished him good luck, and he left.

So, for anyone who may read this, just remember the next time you or your friends are refused another drink. Before you give the bar person any grief. Just think about this, it's easy to fire up more drink and get more money in the till. Maybe, just maybe, they are thinking about your safety in getting home, and being responsible about your care.

2013: JAZZ FESTIVAL

The Jazz Festival is certainly one of the highlights in the city, for many years now, and one I looked forward to each year. A chance to hear talent, not available too often. One of my favourites, who regularly played a gig in the bar, was the one and only Cat Scratch Fever. A great bunch of lads, who gave their all, with great humour included.

This particular year, we had a real treat, when James Galway, and his brother, called in for a drink. Then James kindly gave us a song while his brother George, accompanied him on the flute.

On the Sunday night, at the close of the festival, Dee and the Delta Boys were just about to finish their last few numbers. A knock at the front door, and in walks Big Mark Patterson, followed by the Jay Dee Band. This was followed by another knock at the same door. Standing there were Paul McIntyre, and with him, Warren Smith, sax player for Van Morrison, on the Astral Weeks album.

It was a close for a festival, which was something else. Delta Boys on stage, Jay Dee band, all seated around the lounge, with Paul on piano, and Warren, on top of the piano, playing saxophone. The customers singing along to Mac the Knife, it just couldn't get any better.

Thank you all for the memories. When I was thirteen, I played drums in St Mary's Accordion and. I thought then, that it would be hard to feel better about music. My drumming never got any better, but my love of music did.

2013: EGGED ON

Sunday evenings from 6.00pm to 9.00pm, the craic was always great. Over the last number of years the number of regulars had grown. They would be in at 6.00pm, just as a programme on Highland Radio started. The programme was called Unchained Melodies, and it was a mixture of music and songs through the decades. The DJ only gave the name of the singer or musical, after the record finished, so we had a sort of quiz. Sadie, the bar lady, and I would challenge the regulars to a quiz. This contest always produced great banter.

On this Sunday evening, after the quiz, we were talking about films. Denis Hannaway happened to say that one of his favourite films was Cool Hand Luke, starring Paul Newman.

I said, 'I enjoyed the film, but the part that Newman ate two dozen eggs, for a bit, was a bit hard to swallow, sorry about the pun.'

'Not at all,' Denis replied, 'sure I could eat two dozen myself, no bother.'

He was adamant.

'Wise up Denis, nobody could eat that many hard boiled eggs, one after the other.'

'I could,' he said, 'I love them.'

So we left it at that. The following Sunday morning, I was in my local shop, and spotted the eggs. I couldn't resist it. I bought two dozen eggs.

That afternoon, I boiled them, and when they had cooled, I put them in a large glass jug, after I had taken the shells off them, and I filled the jar with cold water and some vinegar.

I headed down to the bar early, and placed the jar under the counter, at the corner of the bar, where Denis usually stood. I told Sadie about the eggs, and we could not wait for the gang to arrive. Sure enough by six, they were all there.

We had the quiz as normal, and then started chatting about different topics. One of the regulars brought up about a good film he had seen, due to me having a word in his ear, before Denis arrived. So that gave me the opening.

I said, to them all, 'What about Denis last week, he told me he could eat two dozen eggs?'

And they all said, 'I'm sure Denis could, he's a big guy, right Denis?'

'I know Joe doesn't believe me,' said Denis, 'but I could, no problem.'

With that, I reached down under the counter and produced the jug, up on the counter.

Denis was very calm, and the chuckles went round the bar.

'Now, before I start what's the liquid in the jar?' he asked.

I smiled at him, 'It's just cold water with vinegar, to keep them fresh,' I said.

'Aw, Joe, I'm so sorry you went to all that trouble to please me, but I can't eat anything that has touched vinegar.'

I was speechless, and the whole bar were now ribbing me, and in stitches. What a side step he had made to get out of his predicament.

Just another day to suck it up, and no better man than big Denis, to catch me out.

A true gentleman, as everyone knows, and a true and trusted friend to me, and my son Kevin.

[Editor's note: Newman actually ate fifty eggs in Cool Hand Luke, ('a nice round number'), so you might have to give Mr Hannaway another go at this.]

2020: JOHN HUME

While writing these stories, I have just learned of the passing of John Hume. John was a welcome visitor to Bennigans on many occasions over the years. He was great company to be with and his knowledge on many subjects was fascinating.

John and my brother Johnny were great friends when they were in the same class when both attended St Columb's College in Bishop Street. Many years later they both received a Papal Knighthood. John received his for peace work in Ireland and Johnny for his charity work for the Catholic Church. The Papal Knighthood is the highest award bestowed on a layperson by the Catholic Church.

No matter how many awards John has received, nor lines written about his efforts for a peaceful and prosperous Ireland, the people of Ireland will never be able to meet the debt owed to John and his wife, Pat.

The loss of John will be felt through the whole of Ireland and many other countries. At this time, thoughts and prayers will be most in our minds for John's wife, Pat and family.

Rest in Peace, John

2020: The End of My Journey

On the fourth of November 2014, my 65th birthday, I handed the keys over to the man who has made Bennigans one of the top venues for great jazz, in the North West, John Leighton. Not only is John a great jazz pianist, but also provides a wide range of musically talented artists, from a wide range of genres. I have no doubt he will take the bar to new heights in the coming years, as he has done already.

Looking back now over my years there, I will always remember, and cherish, some of the greatest days of my working life. Like the impromptu sessions, with Tony Jackson on piano, and calling up Ursula McHugh for a song, and all of us in shock, at this lady's voice singing jazz. A regular visitor to the bar, we did not even know, the talent she was hiding. Now, she is doing shows on a regular basis, and her Star is Born show is a must-see. I saw it a few months ago, in the Playhouse, and was just blown away.

Eamon Friel nights in the bar were something to behold. His songs were magical, and his witty stories just made the night so special.

The Henry Girls launching their CD December Moon. Their songs have, like the girls, travelled the world, and justifiably so.

Billy Bragg, brought in for a pint by Paddy Nash and Diane, and giving us a few songs before he asked to pour his own pint of Guinness.

Marian Bradfield, beautiful singer, guitarist, from Donegal. Her first performance in five years, making a comeback, before heading to the States, for a tour.

Ben Sands, the Mayobridge man. Singer, storyteller, musical, a definite night to remember.

Then the buzz of the band nights. Paddy Nash and the Happy Enchiladas, the Murder Balladeers, John Deery and the Heads, Declan McLaughlin, Glenn Rosborough, Conor McAteer, Conor Mason, Martin Sweeney, for his help in Eamon Friel's night, Paul Casey, Noella Hutton, Soak, Susie Blue, Betty Harrigan, Victoria Geelan, Carol Henderson, Laura and Dan, and a special thanks to One for the Road, who had the dance floor packed, when they played at my son, Brian's, wedding.

And who could ever forget Jeanette and Rory's wedding day, when they gave us a memorable performance of Whole Lot of Rosie and At Last. Jeanette looking stunning in her dress.

Then we have the people who first got the music started in the bar, weekly. Jackie and her late father, John McCready, Horizon, Venice, Don Murray, Mena Bradley, Maggie G, Sharon Nixon, Paul Gallagher, and Eugene McAuley. Thanks to John Ross, for all the open mic nights. Then the one-off nights, which were special occasions. Farrell Stafford, Grammy-award winning trumpeter, Jason Robello, pianist with Sting. Neil Cowley, who, as many witnessed during the City of Culture, is not just a great musician, but a real gentleman, of the highest degree. Jamie Callum, who was so down to earth during the production of his show from Bennigans. Jamie and Neil, in the one piano bar. A dream come true for me.

A special thank you, to each of you all, for the music, support, enjoyment, and care, you all brought to myself, and everyone in the bar.

Thank you also to all the many friends I have met, working behind a bar, especially Sadie Phillips, and Loretta Kennedy, and my bar buddy, Newell McBride. The nights the four of us spent together, behind the bar, were the best.

To the Henderson family, for their support in every break down with music and sound, also their stories and craic on many occasions.

For those who, on many charity nights, provided the free food, especially Cathy O'Donnell, and family.

To Kevin McCafferty, who, when I need a van man, never let me down once.

To Kevin Carlin and family, my sincere thanks and gratitude, for the chance to manage the bar. For the support of yourself and your family, and the friendship over the years. I wish you, and John and his family, a prosperous and happy future in the years to follow.

To Ali Magee, my thanks for preparing this manuscript; and my sincere thanks to Garbhan and Joe at Colmcille Press for all their help and advice.

A Barman's Gallery

Outside our house, Brandywell Avenue, c.1958: Nellie McGuinness, Mary Bonnar, Lily Gillen and my mother, Maggie.

Derry Harps (Buncrana Final 1962): Back, from left, J. Cooley, F. Murphy, B. Nelis, P. Donaghey, J. Crossan, G. McGowan and J. McKeever. Front, from left, W. Ferry, D. McElhinney, H. Wade, Paddy Cassidy, Thomas Cassidy and Robert Cassidy.

Above: On Sunday afternoons at the Wolfe Tone Hall, the bandsmen ran a weekly 'Crackerjack' entertainment show for children. I'm pictured centre with blonde hair, in light jumper, clapping my hands; my sister Sadie is two above and one to the left. Also included are Monica Bonnar, Kathleen Quigley, Kathleen Murphy, Tony Quigley, Martin Deane, Bill Keys, Seamus McAnee, John Doherty (barber), Dessie Kane, and a number of the McAdams clann.

Left: My mother Maggie and father Bill pictured in the back yard of our Brandywell Avenue home, c. 1956.

Above left: Pictured in my St Mary's Band days in Bundoran with Catherine Curran, whose sister Emma later married my brother Harry. (Catherine and I were the two main witnesses at the wedding.) Above right: My brother Harry and Denis Hannaway, c. 1958-9.

Foyle Harps F.C. - McAlinden Cup Winners 1963. Foyle Harps team who defeated Wellington Rovers 4-2 in the McAlinden Cup Final at the Brandywell. Back row L to R: W. McMonagle, G. Downey, B. Nelis, J. McKeever, G. Ferguson, G. McGown, J. Moran, W. Meenan. Front row L to R: R. Ballard, J. Doherty, W. Ferry, J. Murphy, J. Brown, J. Crossan.

Billy in his Coleraine FC days.

Back right, my childhood hero, and brother, Billy 'Cran' Nelis, who went onto play for Derry City and Coleraine FC. His Derry Celtic teammate John 'Jobby' Crossan, who later captained Manchester City, is pictured centre.

Our Harry with George Best after a charity match in Tobermore.

Jimmy Liddy (front), Pat McCrossan (fiddle), Ray Jordan (vocals) and Pat McCrossan Junior (who invented the two-headed guitar), pictured at the Roadhouse, where I served my apprenticeship.

With my mother Maggie at a family wedding at the Everglades Hotel.

Paul Molloy, John Feeney and big Willie McCready enjoying a charity night.

Pictured on right with the Desmonds Devils, winners of a civic week competition at Lisnagelvin Leisure Centre.

Garvin Kerr, who started working with me as a 14-year-old in the Derry City Club in the early 1970s, and his wife Marie.

Bennigans regular Kevin O'Donnell, who raised £2,200 for charity, by bravely volunteering for a glider flight at Eglinton and by piloting his wheelchair around a seven-mile lap of Derry's two road bridges.

A photo from a card I received from friends and regulars, the day I took over the lease of Bennigans.

My sister Sadie and my brother-in-law Davy.

Kathleen McMonagle, Busty Quinn and Kathleen Gillespie at William McCready's 40th birthday party.

Eugene McCauley and the late Dai Parkhouse enjoying Eugene's birthday celebrations.

My great friend Newell McBride and his wife Josephine, both now sadly deceased.

My great colleague Sadie Phillips behind the bar at Bennigans.

Bennigans staff pictured 'out the back' after a charity night: Kevin Nelis (son), Michael McGuinness, Sadie Phillips, Newell McBride and yours truly.

Maestro, pianist and frequent compere Tony Jackson with Bennigans regulars Kevin, Adrienne, Anne and David.

Kevin and Lily Carlin, proprietors of Bennigans.

Bennigans Charity Committee handing a cheque for £6,040, the proceeds of a charity function for destitute children in India, to Eamon Melaugh, Action With Effect.

Regulars enjoying Sunday night sausage rolls during the jazz session hosted by John Leighton. (To the right is the late David Holly.)

Don Murray, Brian Liddy and myself performing Tennessee Waltz charity night. Brian, who was originally from Creggan, was twice awarded the Policeman of the Year Award in his adopted home of Cincinnati.

Wedding celebrations at Bennigans for singers Rory O'Doherty and Jeanette Hutton.

Pictured with the legendary jazz musician and BBC presenter Jamie Cullum. He came to Bennigans as part of a series he produced on great piano bars.

Jazz pianist and City of Culture musician-in-residence Neil Cowley performing in Bennigans.

Joe, Jim, Roddy and Billy of One for the Road, who played regularly at Bennigans and at my son Brian's wedding.

Regulars toast the the demolition of the Bennigans outside toilet in 2004: Kevin Donohue, James Duffy, Tommy Carlin (seated), Damien Campbell, and Jimmy Henderson.

Folk Club host Martin Sweeney

Kenny 'the Big Dote' Stevenson and Lexie McGarrigle at the Guildhall fundraiser for Action With Effect.

Siblings together with Johnny (centre) at the Mass at the Church of the Annunciation, Chesterfield, where he received his Papal Knighthood. From left, Harry, Margaret, Sadie and myself.

Father and son, the two Marty Dohertys. Marty Junior, who played with the Murder Balladeers and Paddy Nash & The Happy Enchilidas, was doing a set in the bar, where he was delighted to be joined by his dad. Lorcan Doherty was on hand to capture the picture for posterity.

Deirdre O'Hara and singer Ursula McHugh, during an impromptu Saturday afternoon jazz session.

Damien Healy who worked with me from my Bowery Bar days.

With my brother Jimmy during our Brooke Park Bowling Club days.

My nephew and long-standing Bennigans compere, William McCready.

William McCready and Sadie Phillips, during our 'Can't Sing, Will Sing' staff versus customers fundraiser – the first of many we would host for Action With Effect.

My son Kevin (no tie) and nephew William McCready at the Guildhall charity night.

In 2011, a number of us went to India to support the work being carried out there by Eamon Melaugh's charity Action With Effect. I'm pictured here at the Taj Mahal but my thoughts were still in the leper colony we had just visited.

Behind the bar at Bennigans with my son and 'apprentice' Kevin.

Jean and the late Lexie McGarrigle, pictured at a big Guildhall charity night hosted by Bennigans for Action With Effect.

Proud winner of the Most Responsible Pub or Entertainment Centre at the 2013 Derry Business Awards.

Enjoying a rare night off on the other side of the counter with John Feeney and Busty Quinn.

My late brother-in-law John McCready with the American country star Gene Watson, who visited Bennigans after a barnstorming performance in the Millennium Forum.

My great friend, the musician and BBC broadcaster Eamon Friel, was a regular performer at Bennigans. We are pictured here at a tribute night organised for Eamonn by his fellow musicians at An Chultúrlann in 2015. Eamon passed away in 2019 and there are now plans to erect a statue in his honour.

Enjoying a family night out with my siblings Harry, Sadie and Margaret.

With my lifelong friend John McCormack at his 70th birthday.

Pictured with two regulars and favourites – the BBC presenter Mark Patterson and the late Nobel Laureate John Hume. He and my brother Johnny were great friends at school, both later becoming Papal Knights.

Paul Molloy, Eugene McCauley, Una Dunne and a mystery matador enjoying Halloween night in Bennigans.

The Henry Girls in action in the lounge.

The internationally-renowned Keith Harkin leads the Bennigans session.

Presenting the keys to Bennigans to new leaseholder John Leighton upon my retirement on my 65th birthday in 2014.